Last of the Gnostics

THE END OF THE CATHARS

Mary Magdalene's Gospel Revealed

By

DON DURRETT

(Fifth Edition December 2014)

Library of Congress Control Number: 2010926169

Cover & Book Design by EckoHouse Publishing.

The symbol on the front cover was worn by
Raymond the VI during the Albigensian Crusade.

ISBN: 978-1-4276-5005-4

www.dondurrett.com

I know that God exists. I don't need to believe, I know.

— ***Carl Jung***

I think, therefore I am. No, I am aware that I think, therefore I AM.

— ***Eckhart Tolle***

The triumph of Catholicism was a spiritual and cultural disaster from which we are still recovering.

— ***Timothy Freke & Peter Gandy***

Fundamentalism is a Protestant continuation of the intolerance and dogmatic traditions of Catholicism.

— ***Timothy Freke & Peter Gandy***

The language of Angels is laughter.

— ***Steve Rother***

READERS' REVIEWS

I met Don Durrett when a friend brought him to my home for tea. My wife and I spent several hours listening intently as Don spun out a seemingly unlimited, integrated understanding of metaphysics. We were both astonished at the depth and breadth of his knowledge, the distilled clarity of his explanations, and his obvious sincere commitment to living and breathing his spirituality. Don is a master teacher.

I am a Gnostic—a one who knows or seeks to know God personally, rather than believe in others' accounts of Him. This was also the path of the Gnostic group the Cathars depicted in Don's book, *The Last of the Gnostics.* His book sheds historical light on the incredibly important, ongoing struggle between repressive religious orthodoxy and mysticism. *The Last of the Gnostics* returns us to a time when the Cathars fought a desperate battle with the all-powerful Catholic Church in an attempt to hold open the direct portal to God that Christ had opened to them—to all of us. Perhaps the most important message to be found in Don's book is his personal declaration that now is the time when we will once again embrace the ways of the Cathars, the Gnostic ways, and rediscover that long-hidden direct doorway to God that still stands open to each of us.

- Stephen C. Paul, Ph.D., author of *Illuminations, Inneractions, In Love*, and *Hollow Bones.*

Congratulations on writing a book that will edify so many people regarding the Gnostic philosophy and history of the Cathars. I found this book enlightening, educational and an extraordinary read.

- Orpheus Phylos, author of *Earth, the Cosmos, and You.*

Don,

I have read everything you have written, and loved them all. While reading about the Templar Knights to a friend, we were ushered into a higher realm for 27 minutes. Kat could not believe her eyes, or the things we were privileged to see.

I love the fact that you were "chosen" to write at this time, and I recognize that you have not written by yourself, but by the "Spirit of Truth." What a wonderful "Gift" the Spirit has given us, in you, Don Durrett.

It has been my wish to the Universe that Spirits like you would come to teach with Integrity the Truths without "Fear." Like a small child at Christmas, I have been anxiously waiting the opening of these "truths/writings" knowing that they are not just for the few, but for the "ALL." My prediction is that your writings will become the new way of life and that every person that intends to survive will need them. It will guide them on their Journey.

I place you in the company of Nostradamus, Cayce, Krishnamurti, and last but certainly not least, Christ Jesus, who is my favorite.

I have known The Spirit of Don Durrett for many lifetimes, as he and I are inseparable. We have chosen to help one another through all Eternity. We are on this Journey together and I want you "ALL" to know that he is "Second to None" ... the Spirit of Christ is within him, as he has Great Love for THE ALL.

I know that Don has willingly given up a great deal to write these truths. I do not believe that there are words on this planet to tell you, Don, how much I respect you and what you are doing for THE ALL. I will Honor and Love You for eternity, Love and Light to ALL.

In Spirit,
Ladyhawk

ACKNOWLEDGEMENTS

Initially, I thought I was writing alone. Then I came to the awareness that I have help. I don't consciously channel. It is much more subtle than that. All I know is the ideas popping into my head are only partly mine; many are coming from the "other side." Thus, I don't take sole credit for these words. I share this book with the Universe, who is my co-writer.

I must give credit to those who helped make this book possible. First, to my editor, Joanna Benz. She has provided me with the final touches that no writer can do without. I feel blessed to have found her. Next, to my close friend, Toni Harper, whom I have relied upon for proofreading, critique and support. Lastly, to my family, friends, and readers. Without their support, I might have given up.

INTRODUCTION

The early Gnostics, especially the Cathars, on whom this book is based, have always held a fascination for me. I've always considered their beliefs closer to Jesus' message than traditional Christianity. For this reason, I think that their historical existence is of substantial significance. Moreover, a careful look at their spirituality can provide insight into the recent proliferation of New Age spirituality, as well as the reason for the coming downfall of traditional Christianity.

Gnosticism is the pursuit of Gnosis. Gnosis, pronounced NO-SIS, is the direct knowledge of God, or more specifically, the direct knowing that we are consciously connected to God. A Gnostic can either have Gnosis, or be in pursuit thereof. (An agnostic is just the opposite: someone who believes that, although God may or may not exist, it is impossible to have true, firsthand knowledge of God.)

As you read this book, you will often find reference to the term "the *nous*." I took this term from Mary Magdalene's Gospel, and it is being used to indicate our spiritual mind, which is also connected to the universal consciousness where we are all connected and all *One*.

There is a large body of historical material that shows that the original Gnostics believed in the interconnectedness of consciousness. The Gnostics were the first people in the West to spiritualize the concept of a direct connection—through our soul—to God. This was a significant development. It was the first step that has allowed us to evolve to the point where we are now ready—as a civilization—to recognize that God exists in everyone and everything.

The Gnostic message of being *directly* connected to God was denied by the Catholic Church, and acceptance of such a belief was labeled as heresy. The first members of the Catholic Church were content to hear the words of Jesus, and to accept priests as their leaders and intermediaries to God.

Whereas the early Catholics denied their connection to God, they did acknowledge Jesus' direct link, which is documented by many scriptures, including "It is not I who perform these miracles, but the Father," and "Of these things I do you can do as well, and even greater." From these teachings, the Gnostics recognized that they, too, were directly linked to God, and so they felt no need for religious leaders and intermediaries.

Today, more and more people are finding spirituality on their own, using a direct connection with God. Most of these people have no idea that they are Gnostics and that their beliefs are affecting everyone. Gnosticism is changing civilization, as more and more people realize that we are all connected. There is a steadily growing awareness that all of humankind is *one*, a complete consciousness that is interconnected and interrelated. Humanity is starting to recognize that we all share the same source, the same consciousness. This is the very thing that the early Gnostics tried to instill.

The time for society to accept this revolutionary idea is drawing near. We are approaching a moment in history when humanity will acknowledge that God exists in all things, and that God *is* all things. For this reason, I am writing to honor the last organized Gnostics—the Cathars—who were murdered for their unwavering belief in Gnosis. Without their efforts, we may not have reached this opportunity. Their story needs to be told, and we need to remember their contribution.

Don Durrett

October 28, 2014

AUTHOR'S NOTE

This is a historical novel, and the story was based on historical facts or, in some places, inspired by them. Every battle and the dates of the battles are true. Raymond VI, Raymond VII, Simon de Montfort, Arnaud Amaury, the Popes and the Kings of France mentioned, are all historical people. While there is no prophecy in Mary Magdalene's Gospel, all of the other references are fact, except the rules of love and living—I made those up.

Blanche of Laurac did own a castle in Laurac during the Albigensian Crusade, and she was known for her support of the Cathars. However, she did not have a daughter named Joanna. She actually became a Perfecti herself, after the crusade began, and died at Montségur. I gave her a pivotal role in this story to honor her courage. As a noblewoman, she gave up everything to become a Perfecti, knowing that it would, most likely, lead to her death.

The Cathars, and the feminine aspect of Christianity that they represented, need to be remembered and honored. I think that they embodied something that is very important, perhaps even the key to our future spirituality. They represented the purity of love, and how love binds us all together. More than that, I think they understood the importance of love and what it represented to the soul.

To have met a Cathar Perfecti in Languedoc, before the Albigensian Crusade began, was to meet someone who represented the epitome of love. They were the pure ones. They were called les bons hommes and les bons femmes (the good men and the good women). They lived by very high ideals and were the true followers of Jesus. They were Christians who balanced the masculine and the feminine, treating both sexes equally—something that we are still striving to achieve today.

If the Catholic Church does fall—and I think there will be only two more Popes—it will most likely be replaced by a non-organizational form of Christian Gnosticism. Something very much like the individualized beliefs of the Cathars. People will find their spirituality from within, and not through the dogma of any organized church.

* * * * *

Today our culture focuses on economics, on money—and love is relegated to family and relationship issues. But I believe that what Jesus put in motion is about to culminate. His message that "Love is the only answer to the human existence" is about to be accepted. I'm not sure when this change will occur, but it will be during our lifetime.

Currently, as a civilization, we perceive ourselves to be separate from one another. For this reason, we have neglected Jesus' message and have become an incredibly materialistic society. Soon we are going to begin recognizing our inherent connection and the fact that everything is interconnected. This will create the transformation of humanity and the culmination of Jesus' mission.

The Cathars are a link to the past and a history that we can use to make the "jump" in awareness. Anyone can read this book and "get it." Hopefully, it helps people understand how Jesus' message was misinterpreted by the early Catholics, and why Christianity went astray.

The Gnostics were literally burned at that stake, and Jesus' true message went with them. From the time of the Cathars extinction until today, we have not had a true group of people who represented Jesus' message. For this reason, I felt compelled to tell their story.

After years of thinking about the Gnostics, once I sat down to write about them, the entire story came to me. I am more passionate about this book than my others for this reason. It came from deep inside of me.

One of my motives for writing this book is that I believe that I am in some way connected to them in a previous lifetime. I feel that, in many ways, I am writing this to honor myself and the many thousands alive today who also have had past lives as Gnostics. Those lives were not spent in vain, and those contributions need to be honored.

* * * * *

I used the feminine as the basis for the plot. It begins with three women disciples: Mary Magdalene, Mariam, and Sarah traveling to France at Jesus' request to spread the true message. Then the story follows three more women: Margaret, Blanche, and Joanna. Intertwined with them is Mary Magdalene's Gospel. I did this on purpose. The feminine has been missing from Christianity, when in fact it was a focal point of Jesus' teaching—love is what binds us together.

Today, the modern day Gnostics are mostly unknown women. For this reason, I did not give any of the girls—whom Joanna taught—names. They are nameless for a purpose—to show how anonymous New Age Gnostic women are today.

At the end of the book, when Montségur falls, I show Joanna and Blanche jumping into the fire. I purposely focus on their deaths to show that it has been women, much more so than men, who have borne the burden of Gnostic spirituality. (It is estimated that 9 million women were burned, mainly by the Holy Inquisition.) I also show that their spirituality allowed Blanche and Joanna to be fearless. It will be fearless Gnostic women who lead the way in the future. Jesus was called the peacemaker, but it will be Gnostic women who show us how to create peace on earth.

Contents

MAP OF LANGUEDOC, 1209

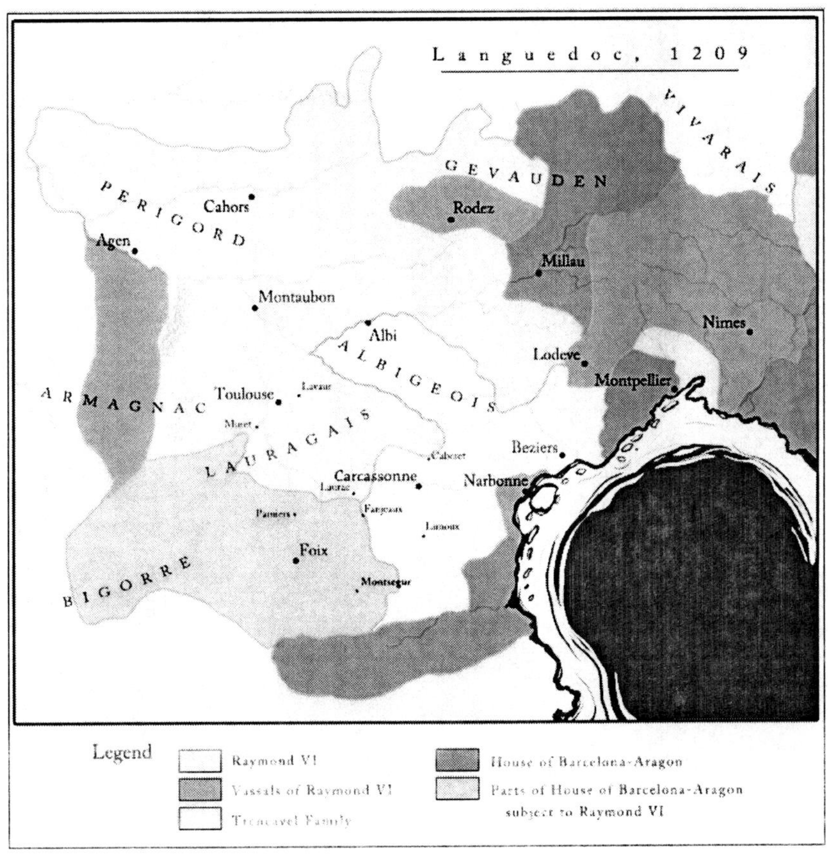

Chapter One

Mary Magdalene's Gospel

As Mary Magdalene walked down to Jesus' tomb, her grief was still apparent on her face. Her lover and husband lay dead after his brutal crucifixion. She was in intense emotional pain, and did not know how it could ever subside.

Suddenly, as she approached the tomb, Jesus appeared right in front of her, as if from nowhere, only a few feet away! She instantly felt their closeness again, and relief from her pain. Her eyes welled up with tears of happiness and she lunged forward to embrace him.

Jesus put up his hand to stop her, but spoke gently. "Stand back, Mary. I am in spirit now. You cannot feel me."

Her emotions were still raging. She was disappointed that she could not hug him, yet overjoyed to see him again.

"Have you been to the Kingdom yet?" she asked, with tears flooding down her cheeks.

He nodded, with a joyful grin. "Yes, it is so beautiful. Don't worry, we will be together again. You have nothing to fear."

"I miss you."

"I know, but you have to be strong. Now is the time for you to perform your mission."

Mary Magdalene looked puzzled. "What do you mean?"

"I need you to leave and go to France, to live with the Essenes. It's no longer safe here. Have your father take you, and also bring

Sarah and Mariam. The three of you are to spread my message in France. What you start will last for generations. Then it will die, but it will be reborn in the end times."

"Why us three, Yeshua?"

"It's your destiny. All of you are highly evolved like myself. The three of you are to write The Book of Love. I won't be there to help you write it, but know that I will help inspire you from the other side."

"And what about the Apostles?" she asked quizzically. "Won't they also spread your message?"

"Yes, and they will succeed in starting a new church. A universal church that will spread and eventually become the Church of Rome."

Mary suddenly became confused. "Why them? Why should they start a church? They don't understand your message."

"It is how it has to be, for now. In the end times, this church will eventually fall, to be replaced by yours. Your mission will lead to the correct outcome. People are not yet ready to recognize that we are all God, and that purity is the pathway to enlightenment. It will take generations, millennia. Your mission is to not let my message die."

Now Mary looked almost afraid. "How can we do this? It is such a burden."

Jesus grinned. "The Essenes will help. I need you to tell the people of Languedoc what you know. Don't keep your wisdom to yourself. Write The Book of Love and share it with the people. Trust me, in the end times, it will have a much larger impact than Peter's Church of Rome. It will impact the entire world. His church will fall and yours will rise."

Mary was crying again, but she was also feeling consoled and joyous. "You want me to teach about the *nous*?"

He nodded. "Yes! Teach the Essene Perfecti in Languedoc. They will help you spread the message. Tell them that I sent you."

Jesus' spirit body began to slowly dissolve into the ethers.

"Don't go! Will I see you again?"

She waited for his reply, but the visitation had ended. Once more, she felt her terrible loss. Then she fell to her knees in desperation and cried.

* * * * *

Mary made the thirty-mile journey to the Essene community at Mount Carmel, northwest of Jerusalem on the Mediterranean coast. Her meeting with Jesus had consoled her, and the intensity of her grieving had somewhat diminished. She gathered her strength, knowing that she must lead the others to France. She was Joseph of Arimathea's daughter and the strongest of the women disciples.[1]

Walking through the gates, the first person she saw was Anna, Jesus' grandmother, one of the spiritual leaders of the community. She walked to Anna, who was on her hands and knees, tending to the garden.

"I just saw Yeshua! He spoke to me!"

Anna looked up at Mary in her normal serious gaze. "Did he give you a message?"

Mary nodded.

"Let's go inside and talk." Anna rose and dusted off her clothes.

Mary smiled. "I'll go get Sarah and Mariam and meet you in your room."

The four most important women in Jesus' life all sat comfortably in Anna's room. This was where Jesus had spent many hours talking with his grandmother about the ways of God.

Mary Magdalene looked at Sarah and Mariam. "I saw Yeshua this morning, near his tomb, and he gave me a message!"

---

1 *Anna, Grandmother of Jesus*, Claire Heartsong, S.E.E. Publishing, 2002, p. 128.

Sarah and Mariam stared at her with wide-eyed, shocked expressions, waiting for Mary to continue.

"He said that we have to go to France, to Sarah's home, with the Essenes. He said for us to write The Book of Love and teach the Perfecti what we know, and have them help us spread his message."

"Why not here?" Mariam asked thoughtfully.

"He said this is how it has to be, because people here are not ready to recognize their divinity. We are to spread the message in France, and Peter and the Apostles are to spread it here."

"Most of the Apostles are feeble minded," Sarah said. "What message can they spread?"

"Now, we don't need to call them names," Anna said. "These are the men that Yeshua selected to be his Apostles. They have a role to play."

"I'm sorry," Sarah said.

Anna looked at Mary. "Anything else?"

"Yes. He said that Peter and the Apostles would create a new church. Peter's church is going to become the Church of Rome. It will eventually fall because it will not include his true message."

"And what happens to the message that we deliver in France?" Sarah asked.

"It will die at the hands of the Church of Rome. However," Mary grinned, "it will be reborn in the end times, and will replace Peter's Church, impacting the entire world."

"The end times? When are the end times?" Mariam asked.

"Yeshua said millennia from now," Mary replied. "That means at least a thousand years."

"Let me see if I understand," Sarah replied. "The three of us are going to write a Book of Love that could possibly inspire a new church based on Yeshua's true teachings. Then it is going to be destroyed by the Church of Rome, only to be reborn and become the world's religion in the end times?"

Mary nodded.

There was silence. Everyone deferred to Anna to ask the next question. Anna stared at Mary, contemplating what needed to be done.

"Okay, Yeshua wants the three of you to make sure that his true message is not lost. You're the only three who understand it and can write it down with clarity. You need to travel to France and fulfill his request. Joseph will take you in one of his boats. There is no time to waste. You must leave as soon as Joseph can make the arrangements."

Anna looked at Mary. "Tomorrow you need to tell the Apostles that you saw Yeshua. This is of huge historical importance. Do not tell them what he said or where you are going. There could be danger to your travel plans, so it will be better if we are discreet."

Mary, Sarah, and Mariam all nodded in agreement.

"Did you tell anyone that you saw Yeshua?" Anna asked Mary.

"No, I came straight here."

Anna nodded.

They continued to discuss the details of their trip as the night progressed, and also talked about which of the Essene disciples would travel with them.

* * * * *

The next day, Mary, Sarah, and Mariam walked to the Apostle John's house in Jerusalem. All three were first cousins and granddaughters of Anna.[2] Of Anna's children, Joseph of Arimathea was the oldest, and Mother Mary was the youngest.[3] Mary Magdalene was the daughter of Joseph of Arimathea; Sarah, the daughter of Isaac; and Mariam, the daughter of Rebekah.[4]

2 Ibid, p. 128.
3 Ibid., p. 66, 94.
4 Ibid., p. 128.

The three granddaughters were the closest people to Jesus, although Anna was one of Jesus' teachers and he was very close to her, as well. Amazingly, all three girls were born in the same year as Jesus.[5] Not only were they Jesus' first cousins; they were highly evolved souls and spiritual adepts. They could converse with Jesus on a level that was beyond that of the Apostles, or nearly anyone of that era. In many respects, they were Jesus' spiritual equals.

As they approached John's house, Mary knocked on the door and Phillip answered, smiling. "Come in! We've been looking for you."

Phillip was one of the few Apostles who respected Mary and deferred to her understanding of Jesus' message.

"Why?" Mary asked, walking into the house, with Sarah and Mariam following.

"Peter, John, and James saw Yeshua yesterday near the tomb. He told them that he saw you first."

Nine of the twelve original Apostles were present. Thaddaeus and Matthias had left Jerusalem, fearful of persecution. The twelfth, Judas, had hanged himself after the crucifixion.

Peter was the leader of the Apostles and had always been antagonistic towards the women. They did not like to be in his company. In fact, they wouldn't have come today if it could have been avoided.

As usual, Peter was confrontational. "What did Yeshua tell you?" Peter asked Mary accusingly, as the three women were seated.

"Only that I had nothing to fear, and that we would be together again in God's Kingdom."

"We want to hear more," Peter replied sternly. "Not about what he said yesterday, but about what he told you in secret.

5 Ibid., p. 128.

We know that he told you things that he kept from us. You are like him. You understood his ways."

Mary was quite surprised. In the past, they had never shown any willingness or wanted to talk about the inner mysteries. Several of them had even commented that it was sorcery.

"If that is what you want, then I can tell you," Mary said softly.

All of the Apostles nodded in agreement: Peter, Simon, John, James (John's brother), Phillip, Bartholomew, Thomas, Matthew and James.

"Before I begin, I would like to know what Jesus told you at the tomb."

"He told us to spread his message." Peter replied. "To take his place and to spread the good news of God's Kingdom. He said that it is our duty as Apostles."

Sarah rolled her eyes, but didn't say what was on her mind.

Mary nodded.

"All right then. I will tell you what he told me about our demons." She paused for a moment before continuing, to make sure that they really wanted to hear this.

"The first demon is darkness. Without a connection to the Holy Spirit—the *nous*—we live in darkness. With a connection to the *nous*, light enters our soul. The stronger this connection becomes, the more light that we shine. We become light beings, and our spirit shines brightly. For those with eyes to see, this light is magnificent."

"This is utter nonsense!" Peter exclaimed. "Why would the Lord say such things? I have never heard anything like this before."

"I, for one, don't believe he said it," Andrew added.

"Nor do I," Simon quickly interjected in a loud voice.

"Calm down," John said. "These are the teachings of the Essenes. Are not most of Jesus' family Essenes? Was not Jesus taught at Qumran and Mount Carmel? Does he not visit there often? Maybe he just never taught us the ways of the Essenes."

There was confused silence and resentful tension in the room. Peter, Andrew, and Simon really did not want to listen to the *women*. But the other Apostles were not as antagonistic.

"Was not Mary the closest to Yeshua?" Phillip implored. "Did he not speak to her the most? If anyone knows him, it is her. Let her finish, and then we can discuss this matter among ourselves. We did agree to hear what she had to say."

Stony silence prevailed, but Phillip nodded for Mary to continue, so she went on.

"The second demon is craving. Here we do not recognize our soul, so we crave a connection with God. We feel alone, abandoned and neglected—when in fact, God is always with us. Our craving is misguided. The illusion of separation from God is false. We are not separate from God, but intricately connected."

Peter scanned the other Apostles, wanting to stop her from lecturing them. His eyes held anger and a complete lack of understanding about what she was talking about. But somehow he remained silent, and allowed her to continue.

"The third demon is ignorance. Here the ego, thinking it is real, creates mischief. The ego, being ignorant, does not know that the soul is available for guidance. Ignoring the soul, the ego uses experience and memories to find its way in life. The ego is limited to past experience for its decisions. These thoughts from the ego lead one astray. The ego is the mischief-maker, the beginning of all misery. Only a quiet mind—and a connection to the *nous*—can lead one to peace.

"The fourth demon is jealousy. Here we are jealous of God. Overcoming ignorance, we have found the soul. However, we have also found that our identity is threatened. We have discovered that the "me" of the ego does not really exist! All that exists is God—one consciousness that we all share. To overcome this jealousy, we have to give up our illusion of personal identity and become one with God.

"The fifth demon is enslavement to the body. As our jealousy begins to fade, the body continues to seek pleasure. This can be the simple fact of feeling alive, to the more habitual practices of eating, drinking, and sexuality. Feeling and thinking that we are the body must be replaced by the recognition that we are the soul, that we are literally consciousness itself. Then we can begin to feed the soul and not the body.

"The sixth demon is intoxicated wisdom. After we have battled with the preceding five demons, we have achieved a level of spiritual wisdom that is beyond what we have previously obtained. Now we have Gnosis—knowledge of God. This leads us to ignore God and instead play God. We voice our knowledge to the masses, exclaiming our virtue and wisdom. We feel spiritual. We feel god-like. In time, this is overcome, as we recognize our folly and submit to the true will of God.

"The last demon is guileful wisdom. Here we are near enlightenment. We are spiritual beings by this point, with Gnosis, and at the edge of melding with God. But we don't want to let our individuality go quite yet. We don't want to be completely consumed by God. Our ego has one last splurge of individuality. We use our guileful wisdom to keep God at bay, refusing to surrender to the inevitable. Here we are quiet, making our final preparations for enlightenment."

Mary stopped and glanced at the Apostles. "That's it."

"What exactly does all that mean?" Matthew asked, completely confused.

Mary answered quickly. "It takes lifetimes, but, in time, we overcome these demons and find our connection with God. In the end, we become enlightened—one with God. That is what Jesus attained, and it is our ultimate goal as well. Life is a spiritual journey to find God by overcoming our demons."

"Mary," Phillip asked, "Yeshua said that he cast out all seven of your demons. Does that mean that you are also enlightened?"

Mary grinned. "Yeshua is enlightened. I am still on my journey."

"This is blasphemy," Peter interjected. "I've heard enough. These are not the words of Yeshua."

"Would you like to hear his actual words?" Mary asked. "His explanation of enlightenment?"

"Hrrmp," Peter muttered.

"Of course, we would love to hear it," Phillip said.

Mary nodded. "That which oppressed me has been slain; that which encircled me has vanished; my craving has faded; I am freed from my ignorance. I left the world with the aid of another world. Henceforth, I travel toward Repose, where time rests in the Eternity of Time; I go now into Silence."[6]

"What does that mean?" Phillip asked, suddenly bewildered.

Mary answered quickly. "It discusses how the demons have been slain using the connection to the *nous*. The *nous* is the connector between this world and the world of the Kingdom. The *nous* is the stillness of our consciousness—it is the silence. We are not the voice in our head, but the *awareness* of that voice. That awareness is our soul, which is the *nous*. The *nous* is where God is found.

"Once this connection has been established, time stands still. It is silence of the mind that opens this connection. The quiet mind keeps the mischief maker—the ego—at bay. It allows purity and innocence and love to blossom. It is the goal of all. It is the outcome that we all seek. And it is found through the *nous*, which is our soul's connection to God."

"That is beautiful," Thomas said.

Mary smiled.

6 *Gospel of Mary Magdalene*, Jean-Yves Leloup, Inner Traditions, 2002, p. 16-17.

But the other Apostles were not convinced. "I don't understand a word of it," Andrew said.

"It is simply nonsense," Peter reiterated.

Mary rose. "I'm sorry, but we have to leave now. My daughter is waiting across town. I want to get there before dark."

The Apostles rose and nodded their goodbyes. Phillip was the only one smiling as Mary, Sarah, and Mariam left. It had been an uncomfortable discussion, but one that needed to take place. The chasm between the Gnostics and the Catholics was now established.

As they walked away, Sarah said, "I'm glad we don't have to see them again. They wouldn't know the *nous* if it hit them over the head."

They all laughed.

"Phillip, Thomas, and John understand," Mariam said. "I've discussed it with them several times. I wish we could take them with us."

"No, they can't come," Mary replied. "Jesus was very specific. The Apostles are to remain here to help Peter establish his church."

* * * * *

A few days later, they made the short journey from Mount Carmel to the Mediterranean port where Joseph's boat awaited. There were many who were moving to France. Of course, there was Mary Magdalene, along with her daughter Sarah.

Mariam and Sarah were traveling with their disciple husbands, Nathan and Philip, while Jesus' grandmother, Anna, and Mother Mary came with children Ruth, John, Esther and Matteas. Joseph of Arimathea accompanied his grown daughters Lois and Martha, and their husbands Daniel and Lazarus. Myriam of Tyana and her three children Joses, Miriam and Johannes also were making the trek.[7]

After some deliberation, Joseph of Arimathea had decided to go along on the journey. He was getting old and realized that he might not see his daughters again. Also, he knew that this was a traumatic voyage for them, and he wanted them to feel safe. His presence gave everyone a sense of comfort. He was the wise man of the family, the patriarch. He was the one man to whom even Jesus deferred. In fact, his wealth and prestige were of such significance that nearly everyone in Jerusalem knew of him.

7 *Anna, The Voice of the Magdalenes*, Claire Heartsong, S.E.E. Publishing, 2010, p 367.

CHAPTER TWO

The Essenes in France

The group arrived in Provence, on the Mediterranean coast, in April, 32 AD.[8]

Today this is known as the coastal town of Saint Maries de la Mer, in southern France. As the name implies, it was named after Mary Magdalene.

There is an old church in Saint Maries called The Black Madonna Sarah Church, which was built to honor Sarah, Mary Magdalene's first cousin. Sarah had an Egyptian mother, giving her a dark complexion.[9] This could be the reason for the black Madonnas located throughout Europe, one of which can be found, today, at this church. Another reason, which is more likely, is that the black Madonnas represent Isis. She was the Egyptian female archetype that represented the divine feminine.

Saint Maries de la Mer is near present day Saint Maximin Le Saint Baume. Every year on July 22nd—the date of Mary Magdalene's death—people celebrate the Feast of Mary Magdalene. Her skull is removed from her tomb inside Saint Maximin Cathedral and paraded around the city. This celebration dates back to the Middle Ages. It's a fascinating coincidence that the date the Albigensian Crusade began, with its invasion

8 *Anna, Voice of the Magdalenes*, Claire Heartsong, S.E.E. Publishing, 2010, p. 367. This date is according to the modern English calendar.

9 Ibid., p. 154.

of Béziers, was on July 22nd. Did the Catholic Church pick this date on purpose?

Also of historical note, many Christian scholars consider Saint Maximin Le Saint Baume to be the third most important Christian historical site, after Jerusalem and Rome. It has this honor for one reason and one reason alone—Mary Magdalene. Today, thousands of pilgrims from all over the world continuously stream into this city to honor her. Whereas it is not generally acknowledged that Mary Magdalene moved to France, the people of southern France have no doubts and the historical evidence is overwhelming.

* * * * *

Joseph of Arimathea acquired supplies, mules and wagons using his local contacts. Then the group made their way south towards the Languedoc region.[10] This is where Sarah grew up, and she knew the area well. Her father Issac and uncle Jacob (Anna's sons) were the patriarch's of the Essene community at Mount Bugarach. They followed the Roman roads, passing through present day Narbonne, Carcassonne, and Limoux until they reached the commune at Mount Bugarach (which was located near present day Montségur).

When they walked through the gates, Sarah was immediately recognized, and several people ran to greet her. The arriving visitors were joyously welcomed. The community knew that Sarah had gone to Palestine to be a disciple of Jesus. Now she had returned with a husband, Philip, and matured into a strong young lady.

Sarah smiled and greeted her family and friends. Her parents, Isaac (a brother of Mother Mary), and Tabitha (her dark-skinned Egyptian mother),[11] were there to hug her. The children gathered

10 *Anna, Voice of the Magdalenes*, Claire Heartsong, S.E.E. Publishing, 2010, p. 11.

11 Ibid., p. 128, 154.

around her, laughing and giggling. Their friend and teacher had returned.

Sarah introduced the people she had brought with her. When she introduced Mary Magdalene as Jesus' wife and her first cousin, there was awe and silence.

"Where is Yeshua?" one of the younger children asked.

Mary smiled. "He is in God's Kingdom. That is why we came to you. He asked that we come here and spread his message. He told us to come to you!"

There was more silence.

Sarah smiled joyfully. "Oh, we can talk about this later! It's time to eat. Is there any food?"

Everyone smiled, joining Sarah's enthusiasm for life.

"Of course. This way," said one of the Essenes, in a white robe.

The commune knew Jesus. He had visited several years ago. They knew of his special mission and his strong spiritual link to God. He was the walking embodiment of God. A true enlightened one. The Essenes enjoyed spending time with Jesus and learning from him when he visited. They had spent hours talking with him about spirituality. One of the Essenes, John, had known that this day would come, and that Sarah would return after Jesus' persecution. He was ready to help spread Jesus' message.

As in the other Essene communes, all of the Essenes wore colored robes. Each Essene wore the color that matched their spiritual development. Only a few wore white, which was the highest level. It would be the color that Sarah, Mary Magdalene, Mariam, and Myriam (the three Mary's) would wear.

The commune was essentially a school, with a focus on spirituality. The members would rise early, and spend each day in rigorous pursuits of knowledge. They studied spirituality, languages, philosophy, astrology, astronomy, science, history, math and writing. They had an extensive library, much of it provided by Joseph of Arimathea.

Some of their ancient writings were hundreds of years old. The various Essene communities located throughout the Mediterranean area would copy their texts and would share them with each other. Joseph's fleet of ships made the transferring relatively easy.

There were over two hundred people in this community, but only nineteen of them had achieved the highest level, and were allowed to wear white. These nineteen met with Sarah, Mary Magdalene, Mariam, and Myriam to hear the words that Jesus had related to his wife.

Mary told them why they had come, and asked for their assistance in spreading the message. The Essenes understood that Jesus' message would be spread either by them or, eventually, by the Apostles or their acolytes. And they understood how important it was that the correct message be revealed.

"We should do it in pairs," Mary Magdalene said. "One man and one woman. This is what he would have wanted. To show that we are equals."

"Yes, that is how it shall be done," one of the Essenes acknowledged. "We have eleven men and eleven women."

"I will write a Gospel and we can share it with the people," Mary said.

"That is a glorious idea," replied an Essene.

"And only the highest Essenses shall preach the message," Mary said. "Only those with a pure heart and innocence. Only those who deserve such an honor. They will represent Yeshua. They will be his true apostles."

"So shall it be," acknowledged another.

The arrival of Sarah, Mary, Mariam, and Myriam in Mount Bugarach was an incredible event. That night, a major change occurred in the lives of the Essenes. They decided that they would spread Jesus' message so that it would not die with him. This was counter to their normal pursuits from within the confines of their small community. Now they were going to leave the protection of their walls, to go out and actually spread the word.

* * * * *

A few days passed, and Sarah could wait no longer to leave the commune and preach the message. At breakfast, one of the Essenes blessed the vegetarian food, and then they all said the Lord's Prayer. This had become a new custom, instigated by Mary Magdalene. Some of the Essenes had also begun to say the Prayer before going to bed.

"I'm going outside today to preach," Sarah announced. "I will be gone for several days, and I plan on living off of the charity of the people."

"But we have not paired up yet," Mary replied, a little startled. "Who will you take with you?"

"I will go," John said, the Essene who had anticipated Sarah's return.

Sarah nodded at him. Her husband, Philip, was jealous, but he knew that he was not ready to spread the word. This was something that was achieved, not given.

Reaching the highest level was not easy to accomplish. One had to be expertly versed in the Law (Hebrew scripture), and had to hold the virtues of honesty, righteousness, justice, loving kindness, and humility. In addition to this, one must have achieved a strong connection to the *nous*, and mastery of the ego. To reach the highest level, one had to join as a novice with a probationary period that lasted up to ten years. New people were tenured up the ranks very slowly, and were made to prove their ability to hold these virtues.

It was not easy being an Essene, for each Essene community was a very strict place to live. Life there was much like being in a cult, in that there was little freedom. Behavior was strictly controlled, and life was highly codified and stringent.

However, there were benefits for these early Gnostics. Everyone was given access to an extensive education, and the opportunity to become a pious devotee of God. Perhaps the greatest benefit of being an Essene was access to their libraries. They had some of the oldest documents known. Scrolls from Plato, Socrates, Pythagoras, and Philo could all be read firsthand.

After breakfast, John and Sarah packed a few belongings and said goodbye to those gathered at the gates. It was an exciting time, the beginning of a new era.

* * * * *

Sarah and John walked back to Carcassonne. They could have stopped in Limoux, which was ten miles north of Mount Bugarach, but Sarah wanted to start in a larger community. Sarah and John were longstanding friends who had known each other while growing up in the Essene community. John was older, now in his forties. And he was now a celibate Essene priest.

When they arrived, there were many people with whom they could converse. Sarah went up to a group of men, wearing her white robe and looking highly conspicuous with her dark complexion.

"Good evening, gentlemen. Have you heard of Jesus?"

"Who?" one of the fishermen replied.

"The son of God, the Hebrew who recently rose from the dead in Palestine after his crucifixion in Jerusalem."

Several of the men laughed. "The son of God himself?"

Sarah nodded. "I walked with him. I was one of his disciples. His wife, Mary Magdalene, now lives here, in the Essene community at Mount Bugarach.

The fishermen became quiet. "Are you both Essene priests from Mount Bugarach?"

They both nodded.

The Essenes were respected and were known as holy people with impeccable morality. They were not liars.

"Word of Jesus has reached this port," one replied. "They say that he performs miracles."

Sarah smiled. "Yes, he did. I witnessed several. However, Jesus is now in God's Kingdom. He rose in spirit on the third day after the recent crucifixion. He appeared to Mary Magdalene and several of the Apostles. He promised that all of us would join him upon our deaths. This is the good news. We *do* live on. Our destiny is to be with Jesus in God's Kingdom."

"How do you *know* that he was the son of God?" one of the fishermen asked.

"He preached it, and he proved it with miracles like nothing ever seen before. I watched him cure cripples, lepers, and the blind. There was nothing beyond his abilities. He even raised my cousin Lazarus from the dead."

Sarah reached into her traveling bag and retrieved a scroll.

"He also proved it with beautiful words of God, like nothing we have ever heard before. Would you like to hear?"

The men nodded.

She began to read. "It is the Father-Mother Creator within me that does the works you see. Likewise, it is the same Creator within you who cares for you day by day.[12]

"If you bring forth what is within you, what you bring forth will save you. If you do not bring forth what is within you, what you do not bring forth will destroy you.[13]

"The Kingdom is inside you, and it is outside you. When you come to know yourselves, then you will be known, and you will realize that you are the sons of the living Father.[14]

12 *Anna, Grandmother of Jesus*, Claire Heartsong, S.E.E. Publishing, 2002, p. 158.

13 *The Gnostic Gospels*, Elaine Pagels, Vintage Publishing, 1979, p. 126.

14 *Ibid.*, p. 128.

Sarah stopped for a moment to comment. "In this next passage, Jesus is warning us not to get too attached to material things.

"Attachment to matter gives rise to passion against nature. Thus trouble arises ... this is why I tell you: 'Be in harmony.' If you are out of balance, take inspiration from manifestations of your true nature."[15]

She stopped again. "Not everyone will understand this," she said, "but your true nature is expressed as that still, small voice within, that voice that always helps us to know what is right."

Sarah continued, "The following are the words he said in my presence at Mount Carmel in Palestine:

"My beloved family and friends, into whose presence I am returned after a long journey, I am now of a man's stature and the Law of One does rest within me, though not all is yet fulfilled. I await the full awakening, when God comes and dwells permanently within my consciousness.[16]

"I also came to know that I was sovereign unto myself, so long as I was aligned and attuned to my omnipotent Creator Source, my mighty I AM. I realized that I was free and not dependent upon another.... I am here on the earth plane to do my Father's will, and to prepare the way so that you may return to the One who is calling you to rest from your soul's long journey."[17]

"These are beautiful words," said one of the fishermen, after she finished. "Is he the Jewish messiah?"

Sarah nodded. "I believe he is, even though the Jews rejected him and had him crucified. I believe God sent him to us to relieve our anxiety and discomfort. Jesus brought us the wisdom to be like him. He taught us how to have Gnosis, to know God. We are all destined for the Kingdom through Gnosis. Our destiny is

---

15 Gospel of Mary Magdalene, p.8.

16 *Anna, Grandmother of Jesus*, Claire Heartsong, S.E.E. Publishing, 2002, p. 209.

17 *Ibid.*, p. 213.

to be with Jesus in the Kingdom – perhaps not after this lifetime, but eventually."

"What are your names?" Sarah asked. "Where do you live? When priests pass through, they can tell you more of Jesus' wisdom."

They gave their names and directions to their homes. Sarah wrote them down with the pen and ink that she had brought in her bag. Sarah and John smiled and thanked them for listening, then they moved on and began speaking to another group.

After a few hours, she had written down over twenty names. One person asked if they needed a place to stay and they gratefully accepted. They lived there for two weeks and preached to the people.

* * * * *

It was the beginning of the Cathar movement. Cathar means "purity" in Greek, and the Cathars were considered the "pure ones." The Cathars adopted the term "Perfecti" to refer to their priests as being perfect, without blemish. This is only one of several things that the Essenes and Cathars had in common. Their diets were nearly identical and they both pursued intense acetic lifestyles in the pursuit of Gnosis.

When she returned to the community, Sarah told the other priests what she had accomplished and how. Her methods were then replicated by the other priests. Steadily, they all began to spread the messages of Jesus and Mary Magdelane, and her Book of Love.

Sarah was quite passionate about her mission and spread the holy word throughout Languedoc and the more populated Provence region to the east. She visited nearly every village and preached. Her legend grew, as more and more people heard of her and of her royal blood. For she was Jesus' first cousin. Her father was Mother Mary's brother, Isaac.[18]

Mary Magdalene also made some pilgrimages of her own, but they were much shorter and less frequent. She preferred to stay close to Mount Bugarach. When people heard that Mary was in Languedoc, they would come and visit her. She had so many visitors that she tended to stay home and preach from within the confines of the community. The Gospel that she wrote did become the basis for much of the preaching. Parts of this Gospel were discovered in Egypt in the late 19*th* century.[19] Her work was titled The Gospel of Mary. The explanation of the seven demons to the apostles (in Chapter One) comes from this Gospel. There are no surviving copies of the Book of Love, although there is substantial proof that it did exist.

Today, in the French regions of Provence and Languedoc, numerous black Madonnas still honor Sarah's memory. They exist because the people of southern France wanted the world to know that the first Christian priest in France was a *woman*.

There is also a festival that honors the Cathars every May 23-25, in Saint Maries de la Mer. It originated during the Middle Ages, and is a tribute to Saint Sarah the Egyptian, also called Sarah Kali, the "Black Queen."

There is no historical proof that Mariam and Myriam even came to Languedoc with Mary Magdalene and Sarah. There wasn't much time to make a historical mark, so it's quite amazing how much of an impact Mary Magdalene and Sarah made.

It should also be noted that the Essenes' history came to an end within one or two generations after Jesus' crucifixion.

18 Ibid., p. 128.

19 It was discovered in Cairo, Egypt in 1896.

CHAPTER THREE

The Cathars

It was the twelfth century. The Cathars were thriving in the Languedoc region of southern France. Languedoc was a large area, approximately a hundred and fifty miles wide (east to west), and eighty miles tall (north to south). It bordered the Mediterranean in the south, and the Bordeaux region in the north. The eastern border was Avignon near the Alps. The western border was close to Toulouse, near the Basque Mountains bordering Spain.

Languedoc was independent from the French Monarchy. It was an assemblage of three territories that were owned by three noble families. Peter II, the King of Aragon, controlled the southwest. Raymond VI, the Count of Toulouse, controlled the west, north, and parts of the east. Roger-Raymond Trencavel, the Count of Béziers, controlled the south and center.

All of these noble families supported the Cathars. This gave the Perfecti legitimacy and fostered respect. In fact, many Perfecti lived in noble homes and castles. They were honored guests, eating with the families and blessing each meal. When there was a death in the family, they were called upon to perform the *consolamentum*, which insured that the dearly departed's soul went to God's Kingdom.

While there were Catholic Churches and priests in the region, most of the populace was anti-clerical and completely ignored the Catholics. Their Cathar heritage was ingrained, and it went back centuries.

The Cathars consisted of the Perfecti and all of their devout supporters, who believed that the Perfecti were the modern day apostles of Jesus. Perfecti would walk in public wearing their plain, unadorned brown robes, carrying a New Testament or a Cathar Bible and preaching to their supporters. Like the original Apostles, they lived without possessions, and depended on the generosity of their supporters.

Perfecti lived simple, ascetic, abstinent lifestyles, in deference and devotion to God. They believed that their ascent to the Kingdom of God—after their death—was dependent upon their morally astute lifestyle. Any deviation would nullify their ascent and lead to another lifetime—reincarnation—to prove their worthiness.

Their piety and devoutness inspired adoration from their supporters. Perfecti were considered to be the Holy Apostles, the "pure ones," delegates from God who were literally without sin. The people held a sense of awe and worship that was similar to what Catholics held for the Pope. They had little respect for their local Catholic priests, when they realized how much closer to God were their Perfecti.

By the late twelfth century, many things had changed since Sarah had made her first pilgrimage to spread Jesus' and Mary Magdalene's messages more than a thousand years earlier. The Essenes no longer existed, although the high ideals of the Essenes lived on with the Perfecti (as did their vegetarian diet). The Perfecti no longer resided in the Essene communes. Some did reside with wealthy families, but many had assumed the wandering lifestyle of the early Apostles. They were the last ones left to spread the true Gnostic teachings of Jesus.

The Essene training to become a Perfecti still existed, although the methods and beliefs had evolved. Becoming a Perfecti was still not an easy thing to attain. It required discipline and training and a long period of mentoring. Most of the pious asceticism still existed, along with the practice of turning their lives over to God. However, the Old Testament was no longer even studied. And Gnosis was now the sole focus of their training.

* * * * *

Jesus had spoken of the spiritual connection with God and the seven demons of Mary Magdalene. This led the Cathar Perfecti to create a type of dualistic spirituality. On the one hand, there was the goodness of God that was our true nature. This goodness of God could only be found by the spiritual connection to God—Gnosis. This was attained by contemplation, prayer, meditation, and studying spiritual philosophy. This was the inner journey of finding God.

They believed that God existed in spirit and not in the material world, where death and impermanence were prevalent. The spirit world is where eternal light, eternal beauty, and eternal harmony existed. The Cathars believed we could join God in the spirit world if we aligned our lives and virtues to those of God.

The flip side of this duality was the material world of matter. They considered matter to be evil. Anything in the world was evil, even the body. The Perfecti interpreted the body to be evil simply because it was not spirit. They believed that the spirit—our soul—was separate from the body and held our true nature. To them, all of earth, all of matter, was evil. It was basically a place of temptation that could lead you astray.

From this simple interpretation, they extrapolated that Satan was the creator and ruler of earth and of all matter. Conversely, the spirit world was good and ruled by God. Moreover, until we devoted ourselves to God, we were mired in the evil of the world. We would incarnate over and over until we found our way to God.

This was their duality. It led them to become celibate, because the flesh was of matter, and thus sinful. To be with God, one had to see the evil nature of flesh. They did not build their own churches, and they claimed that the Catholic Church was Satan's Church, because it was built of matter. It is not known whether they were vegetarians because of their dualist beliefs or because of their Essene heritage.

They had no respect for the Catholic Cross because, not only was it made of matter, but Christ's body that died on it was also of matter. To them, it was the spirit that was of significance, not the body or the cross. They did use the symbol of the equal-sided cross, which to them symbolized the balance of the masculine and feminine.

Of historical note, the original Knights Templar came from Languedoc and had also used this cross. The Templars were known to spit upon the unequal Catholic Cross during their rituals to show their disdain for the Catholic Church. Even during the Albigensian Crusade against the Cathars, the Knights Templar refused to join the papal (Catholic) army.

The Cathars believed that only the Perfecti went to God's Kingdom after death, and that everyone else reincarnated back to Satan's Kingdom of Earth. Whereas the Catholics promised a free ride to God's Kingdom for all Catholics, the Perfecti said "Sorry!" to their supporters. This did not stop the reverence for the Perfecti. Instead, reincarnation became an accepted belief in southern France.

Over time, the Cathar practices regarding salvation had evolved and become much more liberal. By the twelfth century, Perfecti supporters could actually become Perfecti on their deathbeds. This was done through the ritual of the *consolamentum*.

No one knows exactly when the *consolamentum* began being administered to the dying. But it likely had its beginnings in the castles of the nobles, where monetary donations could be expected. It then likely made its way to the Cathar supporters.

This *consolamentum* was one of the reasons the Cathars flourished. For, not only did the people believe that the Perfecti were the legitimate Apostolic successors, but also that they had the power to send people to God's Kingdom. The *consolamentum* was the reason why Perfecti lived in the nobles' castles.

In the twelfth century, the renaissance was coming to life in Europe. The ideas and beliefs of the Cathars were spreading, as more and more people traveled throughout Europe. To combat this, the Catholic Church began burning heretics in large numbers throughout Europe.

In most cases, the local Catholic priest or bishop for a region would inform the local authorities of a heretic. Then the local secular authorities would enforce the will of the Church, and the heretics were burned.

However, the Catholic Church was having trouble finding a way to purge the Cathar heretics in Languedoc. Without help from the nobles, they had no way to enforce heresy accusations.

In 1165, the Cathars were at their pinnacle. There were Perfecti in every village and town throughout Languedoc, numbering into the thousands. In large towns, like Toulouse and Carcassonne, there were hundreds of Perfecti. They were respected, and they walked among the people as God's apostles. They were the humble servants of God, with just one flaw—they weren't Catholics. As such, they were deemed heretics by the most powerful institution in Europe, the Catholic Church.

That same year, the Catholic Church decided to at least make a point that the Cathars in Languedoc were heretics and illegal. They held a council at Lombers Castle, near the town of Albi, in Languedoc. Afterward, they issued an edict, condemning the Cathars as heretics.

The local authorities were supposed to enforce this law, although the Catholic Church knew this would not happen. Still, it was a seminal event in history. It was an omen that revealed the seriousness of the situation, and how the Catholic Church regarded Cathar heresy. It was a clear sign that the Catholics did not want the Cathars to exist, and that they were going to eventually take more serious action.

Once the Catholics showed up in Albi with their signed papers from the Pope, that was the beginning of the end for the Cathars.

For over 1100 years, the Perfecti had lived in harmony with the people of Languedoc, with little interference. They had been Christ's messengers, the living apostles. They were pious, spiritual beings of the first order.

When Bernard of Clairvaux was asked by the Pope to report on the Cathars in the twelfth century, he had this to say: 'If you interrogate them, no one could be more Christian. As to their conversation, nothing can be less reprehensible, and what they speak, they prove by deeds. As for morals of the heretics, they cheat no one, they oppress no one, they strike no one.'[20] It should be noted that no Catholic knew the Cathars better than Bernard of Clairvaux. He was later sainted as Saint Bernard, and is recognized as one of the great men of his time.

The purging of the Cathars in Languedoc would not begin until the Albigensian Crusade in 1209, but the edict had been made. From 1165 until 1209, a period of tension arose. It was no longer business as usual in Languedoc.

The political machinations were being set, and everyone knew it. All you had to do was travel throughout Europe to see that the Catholics were burning heretics elsewhere. It was only a matter of time until the Cathars felt the flames in Languedoc and Provence.

---

20 *Jesus and the Lost Goddess*, Timothy Freke and Peter Gandy, Three Rivers Press, p. 48.

* * * * *

One of the local Perfecti, Pierre, heard about the Albi edict a few days after it had been announced. He was living at a castle with a noble family in the town of Fanjeaux. Fanjeaux was located in the Languedoc region known as Lauragaise. This was the heart of Cathar strength. Nearby towns included Laurac, Saint Felix, Lombers, Montreal, Verfeil, and Toulouse. Toulouse was the largest and most important Cathar city. It was the capital of Catharism.

Lauragaise was a mountainous region with many castles that were strategically placed on hilltops for protection. It was a bastion of strength, and the Catholic Church had little influence there, although their churches existed in the region and some people did attend mass. By tradition, however, the Perfecti held sway over the populace.

Shortly after hearing the news, Pierre joined the noble family for supper in the castle's great room. They sat down at a large rectangle shaped table, placed with an abundance of food. Their silver chalices were filled with the best wine in the world. In addition to the food, the attire of the noble family revealed the wealth of the region. They wore bright clothes that were embroidered with extravagance.

As Pierre stood to recite the Paternoster (The Lord's Prayer), his plain thick brown robe, and leather belt fastened at his waist, revealed the Perfecti's inclination to live a simple life of devotion.

In the Cathar world, only the Perfecti could pray out loud. Thus, to have a Perfecti around to bless meals was considered a blessing of high order. Perfecti lived in many of the castles throughout Languedoc. They also lived with supporters, although by the twelfth century it was not unusual for them to work and live in their own houses. All of them were celibate, which was a requirement.

As Pierre spoke, everyone bowed in prayer. When he finished, everyone said "amen." Then there were smiles, and the feast commenced.

The suppers in Languedoc were more egalitarian than in other parts of the world. At that point in history, southern France was the only place in the world where women were treated as equals with men. It was also the only place where men supplicated themselves on their hands and knees to women Perfecti asking for prayers or the *consolamentum*. It was the only place where women who lacked royalty could inherit land and attain power with standing armies. The power of the feminine was quite strong in this region. In fact, it was stronger here than anywhere else in the world.

"Perfecti Pierre," asked Charles, the Lord of the castle, "what do you make of the edict in Lombers? Are the Perfecti threatened?"

Pierre was more than just a Perfecti. He was a wise man and understood the ways of the world. He was often asked for his counsel by the nobles who visited the castle.

"It is quite unsettling," Pierre replied, in a somber tone. "There have been burnings of Perfecti in Germany and Italy. I'm afraid it is going to come here one day. If the King of France ever supports the Pope, then we are truly threatened."

"Why do you fear the King?" Charles asked, perplexed. "He has never bothered this region before. We are independent."

"It is not the King that I fear," Pierre answered, "but the Pope's ambition. The Pope requires royal power to do his bidding. He is powerless without it."

"Fear not, King Louis the VII is our friend."

Pierre raised his chalice and grinned. "Let us toast that the King will always be our friend."

After the toast, Pierre rose from his chair. "I need to look in on Margaret. Excuse me."

Margaret was Charles' wife and pregnant. Her labor had already begun.

Charles smiled. "If you have time later, come by my chambers. I would like to hear about my new child."

Pierre nodded and walked to the other end of the castle, to Margaret's room. A midwife was already there and labor had progressed. Pierre prayed aloud, entering the room, and then stepped back and watched. Less than an hour later, a new baby girl cried out her first breath. Margaret held her new baby and beamed.

Pierre smiled down at the newborn child in front of him, as he slowly approached the bed.

"Perfecti, please bless Blanche, my sweet Blanche. Hopefully, she will be a Perfecti, like yourself."

Pierre blessed the child, and gazed at the beautiful baby whose eyes were wide open, staring at him.

"Margaret, she is beautiful, like you. I hope to watch her grow up."

"Oh, you will. She is going to be your student."

Pierre smiled. He wanted to tell Margaret that countesses usually don't become Perfecti, but he knew that was a conversation for another time.

"I need to tell Charles about his daughter. Rest, Margaret. I will see you tomorrow."

She smiled.

Pierre strolled down the stone hallway in the castle. It was somewhat dark and chilly, with lanterns burning every ten feet. But his thick robe kept him warm in the cool air of the castle. Once he entered the Lord's chambers, it was much brighter. There was a fire burning in the fireplace, and a whole chandelier of candles. Unlike the hallway, this room had a wooden floor, with expensive wool carpets. The walls were stone, comprised of large bricks.

Charles was sitting in his favorite chair, about ten feet from the fire. He was still wearing his formal attire, a bright red tunic with gold trim. He looked like a Lord.

"My Lord, I come with good news. You have a new daughter. Her name is Blanche."

Charles smiled. "Wonderful. Wonderful. I am grateful that you were here tonight to bless her upon her birth. Please sit."

Pierre sat in one of the comfortable chairs near the fire.

"You know, Perfecti, Margaret is a descendent of Jesus. His bloodline runs through her veins. As a girl, she spent time at the local Perfecti Women's Home here in Fanjeaux. She almost became a Perfecti."

Pierre nodded. "Yes, I know."

It was a home where the local women Perfecti lived, and trained other women and girls to become Perfecti. These training centers did not exist for men. Instead, men were mentored by male Perfecti. These men could be roommates and could travel together. Until the Cathar monastery and fortress at Montségur was built in 1204, aspiring Perfecti men did not have a place to live and train together in Languedoc.

"Margaret is devoted to your cause," Charles continued. "I think she is going to want to place her first daughter in the women's house. She has already said as much. I want you to know that I oppose this, because our new daughter is noble blood. She should marry into another noble house and give birth to a future king."

Pierre nodded. "I will keep your wishes in mind when I counsel Margaret. I will do everything I can to discourage her."

"Thank you, Perfecti."

Pierre stood to leave the room and bowed his head. "My Lord, thank you for your support. Without the nobles, we could not exist."

"Pierre, you know that I am always grateful to have you in this house.... You have nothing to worry about. We will always support the Perfecti."

* * * * *

The next morning, Pierre walked the streets of Fanjeaux. He wore his usual brown robe, tied at the waist with a belt, and most people knew him by sight. Pierre and the other Perfecti would often emulate Jesus and preach in the town centers and other gathering places. They always carried the New Testament or Cather Bible when they walked in public for this purpose. The Cathar Bible was known to only include the first 17 verses of the Gospel of John, plus parts of the Book of Love, as well as other Gnostic Gospels. The Cathars had an intense affinity to the Gospel of John, and believed John the Baptist was a Gnostic. Jesus, Mary Magdalene, and John the Baptist where consider the three chosen ones to bring the message of love to the world.

Most of the people bowed to greet him as he strode past. Then suddenly, a man saw Pierre and came running to him for help.

He immediately supplicated himself on all fours and pleaded, never once looking up. "Perfecti, Perfecti, my mother is dying. She only has hours left. Please come and give her the *consolamentum*. Please, I beg you."

Pierre knew this man and his mother. He knew them as Cathar supporters who attended his public sermons.

Pierre nodded. "You lead the way."

They walked through the streets of Fanjeaux until they arrived at the petitioner's simple wooden home. Pierre entered the house and made his way to the bedroom. The Perfecti's presence made the elderly lady lying in the bed attempt to smile. She was weak, near death, and her smile would not come.

"Can you speak?" Pierre asked. "Are you ready to give yourself to God?"

"Yes, Perfecti. I am ready," she said in a weak voice that was barely audible.

"Do you agree to renounce this world in favor of God's Kingdom?"

"Yes."

"Do you agree to live an ascetic life of praying, fasting and confessing? Only eating vegetables, fruits, nuts, grains, bread, and fish? Never again to eat the flesh of an animal or the byproduct of an animal such as eggs, milk, or cheese?"

"Yes."

"Do you agree to not lie, steal, condemn, harm, or satisfy bodily desires?"

"Yes."

"Do you agree to live like the Apostles and give yourself to God?

"Yes."

"Do you agree to keep these commandments?"

"Yes."

"Do you agree to contemplate the source of your consciousness with a quiet mind, searching for the *nous*, the connection to God?"

"Yes."

"Then let us pray."

Pierre placed his New Testament on the forehead of the elderly woman and began reciting the Lord's Prayer to seal her new role as Perfecti. If the woman knew the words, this would be her one opportunity to, at last, pray aloud. On this occasion, she was too tired, and Pierre said the prayer alone.

After he was finished, he smiled and presented her with his New Testament, which was the custom of the *consolamentum*.

"Perfecti," he said, handing her the bible, "this is yours. Honor it. It is the word of God. Use it for contemplation. You have now been baptized with the Holy Spirit. We will meet again in the Kingdom. Go in peace. Jesus is waiting."

Pierre nodded and left the room. Her son was kneeling in a corner watching in wonder, as he had never before witnessed the *consolamentum*. He followed Pierre out of the room.

"Perfecti, thank you, thank you. I will give a donation to the women's home."

Pierre smiled. "That would be generous. Thank you."

CHAPTER FOUR

Blanche and Pierre

As Margaret had proclaimed, Pierre stayed in the castle and became Blanche's teacher. Pierre had mixed feelings teaching Blanche about Gnostic spirituality. Charles had told him that she was not to become a Perfecti, but Margaret insisted that she learn about God. However, there was a truce between Margaret and Charles. It was decided that Blanche could learn about Gnosticism and then decide if she wanted to become a Perfecti or marry a nobleman.

In 1184, shortly before the fateful day that would decide her future, Blanche met Pierre in the castle's library for her daily teaching. Little did she know that it would be the last time she would listen to Pierre's words with the expectation of becoming a Perfecti.

The library was small, with only a few dozen scrolls. Blanche had read all of them more than once. Her favorite was a Gnostic scroll by Valentinus, which she had been studying since she was sixteen. It was a copy that Pierre had given to the family. Valentinus was a master Gnostic from the second century. The Valentinians had been purged as heretics centuries before in Palestine and Europe. Somehow, one of the Valentinus scrolls had made it to Languedoc and it was copied throughout the region.

Blanche sat at the lone table in the library wearing a colorful dress while waiting for Pierre to arrive. Every morning they met and he gave her lessons to become a Perfecti. There were lanterns on the wall and two candles on the table. The room had a slight pungent smell from the scrolls, which revealed their steady decay. Spread out before her was the Valentinus scroll. She read one line over and over, trying to fathom its meaning.

Pierre entered the room, wearing his brown robe. He smiled cheerfully and sat down across from her. He was middle-aged, with a clean shaven face and receding hairline.

"Good morning, Blanche," he said with his usual sprightly greeting. "Are you ready for a lesson?"

Blanche was a beautiful young woman. She was extremely intelligent and spent many hours in conversation with her father on the ways of the world. While she enjoyed learning about becoming a Perfecti, she had a propensity for wearing nice clothes. This was incongruent with the ascetic nature of the Cathars.

She nodded. "I think I'm starting to understand Valentinus," she said pointing to a stanza in the scroll. "Is he referring to our false ego when he mentions dying to our true self?"

Pierre hesitated. He had brought Blanche along slowly. He knew that there would be plenty of time for her to learn if she decided to become a Perfecti. Something told him inside that her father's wish for her to be married was her destiny. And her personality seemed to be more conducive to being a noblewoman.

Blanche had just turned nineteen and was starting to become a mature woman. He decided that it was time for her to know. If she was really going to have the choice of becoming a Perfecti, then she should know what it meant.

"Valentinus was one of the first master Christian Gnostics. He studied what Jesus had taught and those who came before Jesus, such as Plato, Socrates, Philo, and Pythagoras. All of these great Gnostics taught the same thing, that we are God. This is spelled out in the Gnostic gospels, such as this scripture from the Gospel of Phillip, 'God is the One who is innermost of all.'[21] Or, my favorite, from the Gospel of Thomas, 'Blessed is he who is what he was before he was created.'"[22]

Blanche was puzzled. "What could we have possibly been *before* we were created?"

Pierre did not rush to reply. Instead, he looked into Blanche's eyes and waited for her to understand.

"God?" Blanche asked apprehensively, staring back at him.

"Exactly! What else could we have been? We have always been God. That is the source of our consciousness. This is our true inner self. By contemplating on this source, we can find God—the One that is innermost of all.

"A Gnostic contemplates with a quiet mind, trying to find this innermost place of consciousness. That is where God resides. It is a place that we all share. That is the source of the oneness of life.

"Great avatars of the past have had seminal moments in their lives where they have literally melded with God. In these moments of epiphany they have literally felt the oneness. Once this is achieved the meaning of life becomes quite clear, which is to become closer to our true inner self. That is what this scripture is about. The ego wants you to believe that this world is real and that it is the most important thing in your life. However, there is something that is more real and has more importance, and that is your inner self, which is your soul."

Blanche nodded, looking down at the scripture where her finger still marked the stanza. "How do we kill the ego, and die to this true inner self?"

"By recognizing the duality of life," Pierre replied. "There is the inner world of spirit and there is the external world of matter—the material world in which we live. The world of matter

21 *Gospel of Phillip*, 2.3.68, The Nag Hammadi Library, J. M. Robinson, Harper Collins, 1978.

22 *Gospel of Thomas*, 2.2.19, The Nag Hammadi Library, J. M. Robinson, Harper Collins, 1978.

is false, an illusion. It is completely subjective and relative. There is nothing real about it. Thus, it is the opposite of the eternalness of God. The inner world is absolute goodness and truth. The external world is relative nonsense and evil. For instance, any idea that exists in the external world is relative. This means that there is no right and wrong, and God allows us the free will to choose how to live. There is no judgment from God, because the material world is not based on truth. How can it, when the world is not real?"

Blanche looked up at Pierre in amazement. "That's why you say that this is Satan's world! God is not really here!"

Pierre nodded. "That's the key to Gnosis. Once you recognize that God cannot truly exist in the world of the relative, then you begin to understand that God's reality is somewhere else—in the inner world of the absolute.

"What Valentinus is talking about is a metaphorical death of the false external personality that we identity with. For instance, my persona as Pierre, the Perfecti, is not real. My true identity is much more than just Pierre. For me to find that true identity, I have to metaphorically kill Pierre and become my true inner self."

Blanche looked confused. "Is that possible?"

"Yes, simply by recognizing that my worldly persona is false. It's no different than an actor playing a role in a play. The actor is aware that he is playing a role, but that it is only temporary. After the play is concluded, the role must be discarded for the true identity."

Blanche smiled. "That's easy to understand! I'm not really Blanche! I'm just playing Blanche. Once I die, then I go back to the real me."

Pierre smiled. "Even better, you can go back to the real you while you are alive today. This is done by Gnosis, the awareness of the source of your consciousness. Recognize that your consciousness does not originate in the material world.

Blessed is he who is what he was before he was created. Instead of identifying yourself as Blanche, identify yourself as connected to your soul and connected to God."

Blanche nodded, but Pierre could see that there was still some confusion in her eyes.

"Killing the ego takes lots of work, and for most of us, many lifetimes. Thus, not everyone can truly become a Perfecti in this lifetime. Attaining purity and awareness requires mastery of the ego, which is not easy. The starting point is recognizing the strength of the ego and the objective of the ego, which is to survive. Thus, attaining mastery is a battle of wills between the ego—our false self—and our soul, which is our true self.

"The ego's intentions are opposite of what we are truly here to do. We are here to find God within and become one with that consciousness. The ego's intention is to focus on its individualism, and on its uniqueness. And to make sure that we lose sight of our purity within, the ego uses external pleasures and temptations to keep us as far apart from our true identity as possible.

"The ego achieves its goal with endless chatter and the voice of temptation. The ego is never content, always wanting something in the quest for more security, more happiness, and more satisfaction. Our minds are an endless stream of chatter, seeking something that is missing or necessary in order to be fulfilled. This is how the ego maintains control and keeps God at bay. However, with mastery, we can quiet the mind and listen to God, to our heart. This is where we find true contentment and the source of love. This is where we find purity."

Pierre stopped and waited for her reply.

"I never realized that was the meaning of life. It makes so much sense the way you explain it. Life is all about finding God, about finding our true identity. How marvelous, yet so mystifying. So many have no clue that this is what we are trying to achieve. I'm ready for this quest for purity. Let's read another scripture!"

"Let's," Pierre said excitedly. "Here's another from the Gospel of Thomas. 'Blessed is he who takes his place at the beginning, for he knows in the end he will not experience death.'[23] Do you understand? The beginning is the eternal source. Once you find the source, you no longer need to fear death. At that point, the false self is understood to be just that—false, part of the relative world."

"I think I do understand, Perfecti," Blanche said removing her finger from the stanza. "Without knowledge of the eternal source, or the beginning as Thomas calls it, we are lost, vulnerable, afraid, alone and ignorant. Our false self is at the mercy of Satan. Without the source, we are in complete confusion! The way of the Gnostic is to seek the source. It is literally a journey home, until we find the absolute purity of God. Until then, we are at the mercy of the confusion of life—or as you put it, the utter nonsense of life."

Pierre was stunned. She did understand.

"The Catholics think we are born in sin," Blanche continued, "but actually, we are born in confusion. We can't sin, because the world is relative and subjective. In fact, it's impossible to sin." Blanche hesitated. "But Perfecti, why do you live with such high ideals if there is no sin?"

Pierre smiled at her wisdom. "Very insightful, Blanche. You sound like a Perfecti today. And, yes, you are correct, I do not live a moral life to make God happy. That would be ridiculous, since our consciousness is incorruptible, and God does not judge our behavior. Gnosis is not achieved by obeying God, but by becoming aware of God—our true self. Perfecti live with an uncompromised morality because we are searching for God, who

---

23 *Gospel of Thomas*, 2.2.18, The Nag Hammadi Library, J. M. Robinson, Harper Collins, 1978.

is absolute goodness. If we are already living with a semblance of that goodness, then it will be easier to find, easier to recognize."

Blanche nodded. "That makes sense, but it's ironic." She laughed. "You don't believe in sin, but you still don't sin!"

Pierre smiled. "Yes, it is ironic. What causes people to act badly is a lack of Gnosis—ignorance. From God's perspective, we are immature children that need to learn. I know that it's hard to equate a murderous barbarian to an immature child, but it's true. This is why the scripture says to love our enemies, not the enemies we choose to love, but *all* of our enemies. For they are not truly our enemies, but ourselves. For all is *one*."

Pierre suddenly saw more confusion in Blanche's eyes. "I have another scripture from John 14:10. 'I am not myself the source of the words I speak to you. It is the Father who dwells in me doing his own work.' Now, I ask you, if the Father is within each of us doing his *own* work, how could we possibly sin?"

Blanche nodded. "You make a good argument. If everyone has the same source, which is God, then we are truly all God, acting as one. All of our actions truly come from God, the source. Very interesting."

Pierre nodded. "Let's see if we can remove your doubt and get you to start knowing, which is Gnosis.

"Gnostics believe that we must look at life from two directions simultaneously. This comes from another scripture in the Gospel of Thomas. 'When you see the two as one … then you will enter the Kingdom.'[24]

"Blanche, as I am speaking to you this moment, I am simultaneously aware of both directions of consciousness. In one direction, I am Pierre and teaching you a Gnostic lesson. That consciousness comes from the external world. On the other hand, the source of who I am is watching and listening from the

24 *Gospel of Thomas*, 2.2.22, The Nag Hammadi Library, J. M. Robinson, Harper Collins, 1978.

other side of the veil—from the spirit world. It is consciously aware of everything I am thinking and doing. This Source is not just a bystander collecting information. The Source is also giving information. The more I pay attention to this Source, the more information I receive. Thus, there are two sources of consciousness that meld into one."

Blanche sighed dejectedly. "I was doing so good today. But you just lost me."

Pierre laughed. "Thank God," he said jokingly. "I thought you were going to become a Perfecti today."

Blanche laughed. "I am doing good, aren't I?"

"You could hardly be doing better," Pierre said seriously. She had certainly amazed him today.

Blanche smiled. Let's go longer today. I don't want to wake up and forget what I have learned."

Pierre smiled. "Sure. We have more time. Do you have another question?"

Blanche nodded. "Perfecti, Catholics believe that they receive salvation through the church; Gnostics believe that salvation is achieved through Gnosis. Are Catholics wasting their time, since they will not find Gnosis in the church?"

Pierre shook his head. "Of course not. Nothing is wasted. Gnosis is not achieved in one lifetime. Everyone has their own journey to Gnosis. Catholics are finding salvation, too. It's just going to take them longer than they recognize."

"Perfecti, it doesn't matter what they believe?"

Pierre shook his head. "No. They cannot get lost. Eventually God will lead them home."

He had sparked her sense of wonder again.

"What do you mean?" Blanche asked, intrigued.

"We all have the same source. God is within each of us. To think that you act independently and alone is naïve and ignorant. We all have inner guidance."

"But how could our inner guidance be so corrupted?" Blanche asked.

"Perhaps a scripture from Clement of Alexandria can help. 'All the actions of those possessed by Gnosis are right actions, and the actions of those not possessed by Gnosis are wrong actions.'[25] Remember, Blanche, without Gnosis we are lost, confused."

"You mean that God allows us to be confused, but still guides us towards Gnosis?"

Pierre nodded. "That's exactly how it works. We might think that someone's actions have nothing to do with Gnosis, but God's plan is beyond our comprehension. Everyone is searching for Gnosis in their own way, even if they don't know it."

"That makes sense," Blanche replied in agreement. "That's why people want to be happy, and why everyone is searching for happiness. However, isn't life really a search for Gnosis? And, is it truly possible for someone to be happy without Gnosis?"

"No, not really," Pierre replied. "At least not with the kind of ultimate, serene joy that is possible. Can one truly be happy who is lost, afraid, and confused? That is the situation without Gnosis. This is why we search for happiness. We know that something important is missing in our life. It is a deep mystery of not knowing. So what do we do? We seek diversions that we think will bring us happiness. A wife, a family, work, hobbies, religion. We can use anything as a diversion from the mystery."

Blanche was surprised by the openness from Pierre. "You've never talked to me like this before. I feel like you're telling me the secrets of the universe."

Pierre laughed. "You've earned it. Your knowledge is impressive."

"Okay, one more question for today," Blanche said. "How did you find Gnosis?"

25 Clement of Alexandria, Strom., 7.33.

Pierre whistled. "You're really ambitious today."

Blanche laughed, and then Pierre replied.

"I contemplated the inner source for years. Slowly, my awareness of God deepened, until I was aware that God and I were acting as one. I became aware that I was God, manifesting as consciousness. The source of this was my soul, which resided somewhere else, somewhere in God's Kingdom. This source looked over my shoulder at my behavior and guided me. It watched my every move. My persona as Perfecti Pierre was not truly who I was. My real existence was my soul, which was also present. Coming to know this 'other me' is what led me to Gnosis.

"Our consciousness is really split in two. There is the false persona of Perfecti Pierre, and then there is the true self that is aware of this false persona. They exist as a meld of one, hiding from the uninitiated. However, through contemplation, you can separate them, you can tell them apart. This, of course, is an inner journey, which leads to the revelation that the Source exists. Once you find that Source, it is simply a matter of time until you become aware that the Source is *God*.

"The revelation starts small and increases with time. At first, you only get a glimpse of God, but you know it's there. Over time, it steadily becomes deeper and more ingrained. Someone with deep Gnosis, such as Jesus, has love and compassion for all of humankind. For they know that our consciousness all comes from the same source. This is why those with Gnosis, such as most Perfecti, have compassion for those still caught in ignorance."

Pierre stopped and waited for Blanche to reply.

"I think I understand, Perfecti. When we look out at the world, we are looking with our false self. When we look inward to God, we are looking with our true self."

Pierre smiled. "That's very close, although I could add more to that explanation. We will talk more tomorrow."

Blanche could tell that Pierre was extremely surprised and pleased with her sudden progress on this day. As he beamed warmly at her, she felt his love and appreciation.

Blanche smiled back, proud of her achievement. Little did she know that this would be their last in-depth discussion of Gnosis.

CHAPTER FIVE

The First Omen—1184

In 1184, the Papal Bull of *Ad abolendam* was announced in Rome. This required the local Episcopal clergy – the Catholic Church – to pursue heresy. It became the duty of every diocese to pursue heretics and inform the local secular institutions about the offenders. Most significantly, it required the local clergy to inform their Bishop of any known heretics in their diocese.

The *Ad abolendam* was very effective in purging heretics in Italy and other parts of Europe, but it had little effect in Languedoc. It merely pointed out how little control the Catholic Church had over the Catholic priests in Languedoc, who often were, in fact, Cathar supporters.

It had been nineteen years since the edict at Lombers Castle in Albi. Pierre had been waiting for another move against the Cathars. In fact, he was surprised that the Catholic Church had left Languedoc alone for so long. When he heard of the *Ad abolendam,* he knew that it was the second omen. They weren't going to stop until the Cathars were extinguished.

On that lovely clear evening, Pierre entered the great room for supper apprehensively. Charles – the Lord of Fanjeaux – and his large family were already seated for supper. The servants had just finished placing food on the table. Everyone was wearing brightly colored clothes, and the normal festive atmosphere reigned. On top of a red tablecloth, silver dominated the large rectangular table. There were goblets, plates, trays, knives and forks, all made of silver. There was meat, potatoes, vegetables, wine, and bread in abundant supply.

According to custom, Pierre blessed the food and they all began eating. After the normal pleasantries of the day, the conversation eventually turned to politics.

"Should we worry about the Papal Bull?" Charles asked Pierre.

"Indeed." Pierre replied softly. "The day is approaching."

"What day?" Blanche asked innocently. She was now nineteen, and there were rumors that she was to wed the Lord of Laurac. She preferred to become a Perfecti, but her father had pressured her ever since she was a child not to become one. This wasn't working as her father's intransigence had simply pushed her closer to Pierre. They had spent a great deal of time together, learning the ways of the Perfecti. Charles did not have a problem with this, as long as she married a noble. Blanche's children could always become Perfecti, once her position was firmly set.

"A reckoning is coming," Pierre said solemnly. "Death and bloodshed for Perfecti. Burning at the stake."

Blanche was shocked and horrified. "Why?" she asked shrilly. "Why does such a thing have to happen?"

"Heretics have always been persecuted by the Catholics," Pierre replied. "The Cathars have just been fortunate to have been protected by the nobles. It cannot last forever."

"Why not?" pleaded Blanche, still in shock.

In the same solemn voice, Pierre said, "Because it is written. It is part of our prophecy. The Perfecti will burn and be no more. Then, in the end times, our message will blossom again to affect all of mankind."

"Where did the prophecy come from?" Blanche asked, the fear in her voice still present.

"From Mary Magdalene," Pierre replied solemnly. "It is written in The Book of Love."

"But does it have to be now?" Blanche asked, finally succumbing to tears.

"It doesn't, but the second omen occurred this week. A Papal Bull was recently issued in Rome. Local clergy must identify heretics and report them to local authorities and to their Bishops. Nothing will happen in Languedoc, because most of the bishops here are Cathar supporters. But there will be another omen. The Catholic Church is not going to let us exist much longer. The third omen is coming."

"Oh, my God!" Blanche exclaimed angrily, with tears flowing down her face. "What was the first omen?"

"On the night you were born, your father and I spoke about the Papal Edict of Albi, which had just been issued..."

"In 1165?" Blanche interrupted, incredulous.

Pierre nodded. "Yes, only a few days before you were born. The edict condemned the Cathars as heretics. I told your father that it wouldn't be much longer. For the last nineteen years, I have reminded him how lucky we have been that the Catholics have not been back."

"They're coming for you?" Blanche asked, terrified. "For the Perfecti?" she said, wiping her tears and trembling.

"In time," Pierre replied, still solemn. "It could be one year, or it could be ten. It's impossible to know. However, I do believe the prophecy. I do believe they're coming. We are the only heretics in Europe who have been left alone. Burnings are happening everywhere else."

Blanche starting sobbing again. "I can't believe that they are going to kill Perfecti! You are not heretics. Perfecti are the holy ones! You are the true descendants of the Jesus. Not them!"

"Blanche," Pierre said softly, trying to calm her down, "remember that this world is Satan's. It is an evil place."

Blanche managed to calm herself and stopped crying. "This should not happen," she said in a stern voice. "I have more royal blood than the Pope. Jesus is my ancestor! I am a true descendent. Christ's blood runs through my veins. They have no right to burn me if I become a Perfecti!"

"Well, that cannot happen if you marry the Lord of Laurac," her father interjected.

With strength belying her years, she looked at her father. "Have you no mercy for the Perfecti? Pierre could be burned. They all could be burned. We must do what we can to save them."

"That is my point, Blanche," her father replied stoically. "You need resources to protect the Perfecti. The Lord of Laurac is very wealthy. It will be a good castle for you. You will have a much better chance of helping them as a noble Countess than as a Perfecti. As you know, the Perfecti cannot defend themselves. They cannot shed the blood of their enemy."

Blanche was silent, contemplating. She had become a very intelligent and determined young woman. She wanted to protect the Perfecti. They represented everything to her: her ancestry, her culture, her beliefs. If the Perfecti were threatened, then she knew that she had to protect them.

"Then I will marry the Lord of Laurac," Blanche said, in a determined voice, "and that is that! I have decided. You can inform his family."

Her father smiled with long-sought relief, and picked up his fork. "Very well then, let's eat. The food is getting cold."

Margaret was shaken by the conversation, and by Blanche's sudden decision to marry. She, too, revered the Perfecti. It was her heritage. And she was afraid that Blanche was making the wrong decision. "Are you sure, Blanche? Is this what you truly want?"

Blanche nodded resolutely.

Margaret was the only one that was afraid. Blanche had made her decision and was ready to protect the Perfecti with her life. From this point on, the only emotion anyone would see from her face was determination. Her father was a noble, with his own standing army. And he had never been afraid a day in his life.

Pierre was silent, eating his vegetables. The Perfecti did not honor marriage. They considered it a necessary evil, part of the evil world of Satan and matter. Somehow, over the ages, Mary Magdalene's Gospel had been interpreted so that the Holy Spirit was good, and matter—the physical world—was evil.

This occurred because Mary Magdalene said that Jesus appeared to her in spirit form after he arose on the third day after the crucifixion. Since Jesus did not arise in his physical body, it was determined that the body must be evil.

The Cathars decided that God existed as spirit and, therefore, the spirit was good. Since there was evil in the physical world, it was interpreted to be ruled by Satan. In effect, the Cathars removed God from the physical world and gave it to Satan. Mary knew better, but her interpretation had been lost.

From a Perfecti's perspective, Blanche had just rejected God—the domain of spirit—and instead accepted Satan—the domain of matter. She had the opportunity to become a Perfecti and ensure a place in God's Kingdom after this lifetime. However, he knew that she could come back and become a Perfecti in her next life. Also, there was always the possibility of the *consolamentum* on her deathbed.

* * * * *

It wasn't long before the marriage ceremony took place. Blanche married the Lord of Laurac and, over the next few years, she had two children, a boy and a girl. She was determined to make one of them a Perfecti—to carry on her royal line of blood as an Apostle.

Pierre was beginning to get old, and had moved to Laurac to live with Blanche in her castle. He only ventured out on special occasions to preach sermons to the public. He no longer administered the *consolamentum* or heard confessions from the public. But his wisdom and powerful spirituality were shared with Blanche's family, and his presence made the castle a special place.

Blanche was now a Countess, but she lived close to the doctrines of the Perfecti. She prayed and meditated daily, and she read from the New Testament and from Pierre's ancient Gnostic scrolls. She was a vegetarian, and had stopped having sex after her last child was born.

Her high moral ethics equaled those of the Perfecti. She was generous and helped the city's poor. She also supported the Laurac Perfecti Women's Home. When she visited the women's home, they treated her as a fellow Perfecti. She was a Perfecti in all but name. Little did they know that Christ's family blood actually ran through her veins.

In 1189, two Cistercian Catholic monks wandered into Laurac and began preaching to the people and condemning the Cathars. Blanche heard about it and went to tell Pierre.

"Is this the third omen, Pierre?" she asked.

He shook his head. "No. The next will be another Papal Bull against heresy. The Cistercians are just passing through. No one will listen to them. They are not our fear. Blanche, the only thing that can jeopardize the Cathars is the withholding of support by the nobles. As long as we have their support, we will exist."

Blanche smiled. "I didn't think it was the third omen."

Pierre smiled. "No. We still have more time."

"How do you feel today?" she asked.

"I feel good. Why?"

"Why don't we walk down to the public square, and you can debate the Cistercians? I can bring the women Perfecti, and there are several men Perfecti in training here in Laurac who can come."

Pierre mulled over her request, and he wanted to say no. However, this might be his last time to debate the Catholics, something he had done many times before. Blanche enjoyed watching him debate and wanted the people of Laurac to see a true Perfecti in action. She wanted the people of Laurac to see for themselves the true descendants of Christ.

Finally he spoke. "Okay," he said. "This afternoon we will walk to the square."

Blanche smiled.

* * * * *

When Blanche and Pierre exited the castle gates a few hours later, there were thirty people waiting to walk with them down to the town square. As they walked, more people joined them. By the time they approached the square, a parade of seventy-five people walked in unison, with Blanch and Pierre leading the way—Pierre in his ubiquitous brown robe and Blanche in her regal gown.

A crowd had already assembled at the square, listening to two Cistercian monks. When Pierre and his entourage approached, they stood back and allowed Pierre to enter and approach the monks.

The crowd mumbled in hushed whispers, talking amongst themselves about this unusual and significant event. A sense of quiet awe fell over the crowd, as Pierre approached the monks. Without hesitation, the crowd quickly formed a circle, with Pierre and the two Cistercian monks in the middle.

Pierre held his New Testament in his right hand. His presence and stature resonated throughout the square. Everyone knew Pierre to be one of the wisest Perfecti in the region. The honor and reverence that was held for him was hard to describe. If he asked the crowd to kneel, no one would hesitate.

The young Cistercians didn't have a chance. Pierre was feeling feisty, knowing that one of these young men might be present at his burning in the future!

"You may go first," Pierre said tersely.

One of the Cistercians preached from his Bible, reading from both the Old and New Testaments.

Pierre, keeping his Bible closed, quoted from the New Testament for nearly ten minutes. Then he interpreted a scripture from a Gnostic viewpoint.

"Jesus says, 'It is not I who doeth these works, but the Father *within* me.' And then he says, 'You shall do greater works than these.' Do you understand?" Pierre asked the crowd.

A few people nodded, but there was absolute silence.

"God is within," Pierre roared. "Can it be stated any more simply than that?" Pierre paused and scanned the crowd. "He does not say that you *can* do greater works than these, but that you *shall*. The key here is time. When shall you do these greater works? When will you be like Jesus? This lifetime? Probably not. Then which lifetime will it be? The answer is simple – when you find God within."

Pierre turned and faced the other side of the crowd. "You will never find God in the world. As Jesus told us, God is within. The Holy Spirit is the connection to God. We all have this connection, or else Jesus would not have spoken these words..."

"You heretics," one of the Cistercian interrupted, "are always searching for God, but never finding him. If you want to find God, then join the Catholic Church and come to mass. Jesus Christ will then give you admission to God's Kingdom. That is the only finding that needs to be done!"

"So, I'm a heretic because I'm trying to *find* God?" Pierre asked, incredulous. "And your Church is the only way?"

"Indeed!" replied the monk. "But there's more. You spit on the cross. You call our church the Church of Satan. You dishonor our baptism and sacraments. You claim that Jesus was married. You believe in reincarnation. You're vegetarians. And, let us not forget, you do not honor marriage!"

"A pity," Pierre said shaking his head in disgust. "Let's not forget that we treat women with equality, and that we give an oath to God not to lie, steal, or condemn. I wish I could take that last vow back and condemn you today."

The crowd laughed.

Pierre continued. "If we built a church, it would be the Church of Satan, too. What is made by man is made by Satan. This is why your sacraments are blasphemy. God does not rule the world of matter; it is ruled by Satan. The world of matter is subjective and God only exists as absolute goodness. At least your Saint Paul got it partly right, when he made your priesthood celibate. Flesh is evil, as the body is made of matter. However, Paul's admonition of women, and subsequent purging of the women's priesthood, misinterpreted the spirit of God *within* women. If anyone should be heretics, it should be Catholics, although we do not condemn your church. You may exist. You may continue your sacraments. I just hope that no one attends."

Several people laughed.

"The Cathars should all be rounded up and burned!" the monk exclaimed.

"Maybe you should also kill Jesus' descendants," Pierre replied, knowing people in the crowd were aware that there were descendants of Jesus living in Languedoc. "You should make sure that there is no confusion about who are the true descendants. After all, doesn't your Pope claim his authority from the Apostolic succession? It wouldn't be good for your church if some of Jesus' descendants existed here in Languedoc."

"You bluff. There are no descendants of Jesus," the monk replied.

"As the people know, a Perfecti does not lie. After his crucifixion, Jesus' child came to southern France with their mother, Mary Magdalene. And they weren't the only members of his family who immigrated to Mount Bugarach; there were also cousins. Jesus' line goes back to the Merovingian kings and their arrival in Provence in 32 AD."

"You lie. You need to be burned."

"If I lie, then maybe I should burn. However, Mary Magdalene's words live on. We know our ancestry. Don't tell us what we know and what we don't!"

The people roared in approval.

Pierre raised his arms to calm the crowd. "If the Gospel of Mary Magdalene is false, then maybe the Cathars should burn. It is the foundation of our heritage. But if it is true, and you burn the Cathars, it will be a great injustice. It will be the work of Satan! For those of you who allow it to happen, know that your ancestors will remember. Also, know that in place of the Cathars will be left the Catholics! There will be no more succor, no more blessings from the true descendants. God's apostles will be taken from this region. Like the rest of the world, Languedoc will begin to wither in spiritual decay. The Cathars will be gone!"

Pierre turned from the monks and walked off the square. The crowd parted in silence and let him pass. He walked alone toward the castle. Blanche, and the women and men Perfecti, followed at a short distance. The crowd had been shaken by his final words, and remained quiet until he was gone.

There had been a gradual buildup of tension in the region with the realization that the Cathars were being threatened. There had been reports for the last few years of Perfecti being burned in other countries. And now, Pierre—their own Perfecti—had admonished them to come to his defense. He had requested their courage to not let it happen. More than that, he had threatened them. In essence, he had told them that if they did not help him, all was lost.

CHAPTER SIX

The Third Omen—1199

In 1199, the dreaded third omen appeared. Pope Innocent III, who had become Pope a year earlier, released a Papal Bull in March, 1199.[26] *Vergentis in Senium* was a law against heresy. It was the harshest law to date, and was specifically written for Cathar supporters in Languedoc. The Church claimed the power to confiscate property, possessions, titles, and the ability to inherit. It went so far as to deny people the right to work in certain professions, such as law and medicine, or to serve as notaries. It was not directed at the heretics themselves, but at their supporters. For the Perfecti did not have anything to lose but their lives.

A young Perfecti came to the Laurac Castle and informed Pierre of the Bull. Pierre was now elderly and he no longer left the castle. After he found out, he summoned a meeting with Blanche.

They met in the great room near the fire. This was Pierre's favorite room in the castle. It was the largest, although not so big that it could not be warmed in the winter. Most of the rooms in the castle were small for that very reason. This was the one room where the whole family could congregate and relax. It was the social room, where they spent most of their time in the winter.

26 The year 1199 is interesting using numerology. 1 is new beginnings. 9 is completion. You could say it was the beginning of the end for the Cathars.

The great room, like most of the rooms in the castle, was made of stone walls with a wooden floor and wooden ceiling. Carpets soaked up the heat of the fire and warmed the room. Tapestries on the walls also served the same purpose. It was not an ornate room, although a beautiful coat of arms hung over the fireplace, revealing the stature of the family.

Blanche was seated alone, waiting for Pierre. She was wearing a colorful gown, although, from her perspective, it was just one of her many dresses. Her husband, the Count of Laurac, had died a few years earlier, leaving Blanche a widow. This did not break her heart, as she had never loved him. Her life had always revolved around her children and her support of the Cathars.

Pierre bowed his head. "Countess," he said, taking a seat opposite her.

Blanche nodded. "Pierre," she said, as a welcoming.

Pierre looked haggard. His hair was unkempt and he had not shaven. Blanche was surprised, as he was usually better groomed. Either his age was starting to show, or this was truly important.

"It has happened," Pierre said, solemnly.

After a brief moment of shock, Blanche broke the silence.

"The third omen?" she asked, apprehensively.

He nodded. "The new Pope, Innocent III, released a Bull declaring heresy a crime. There is a long list of punishments. It is really directed at you, the Cathar supporters. If they find you guilty of supporting heretics, they can take away your castle, your title, and all of your lands. If they find one of your children guilty, they can remove their ability to inherit."

Blanche was stunned and nearly gasped. "Do they really have that power in Languedoc?"

"Not yet, and not without King Phillip Augustus' support. They will need the French King's help to threaten the nobles.

You have your own armies. The Church can't fight them without the King's help, or at least his tacit approval."

"Will the King turn on us?" she asked, her voice now calm.

Pierre turned away and coughed, his poor health apparent. "I'm sorry, Blanche. This is it, the third omen. It will come fast now. This new Pope appears to have made this law specifically for Languedoc. Where else are Cathar supporters so strong that you need a law of this magnitude? He seems determined. He will find a way to make an allegiance with the King. I have no doubt this time. This is the end."

Blanche hesitated. "The Papacy has been trying to get the French Monarchy to pressure us for years. Even if there is an alliance between the Pope and the King, the nobles will still support the Cathars. We are the King's vassals, but he cannot tell us what to do regarding the Cathars. We still own these lands. There would have to be a war, Pierre. That is the only way."

Pierre raised his eyebrows, unsure of the answer. "It's hard to say how the Catholics will attack heresy in Languedoc. They are going to want to arrest and burn Perfecti. They could have a Church functionary do this or a local secular group. Either way, for this to succeed, the nobles will have to support their efforts. They will need the nobles to stand down. If the Pope can get the nobles to turn in heretics, the Catholics have won."

Finally, the enormity of the situation hit Blanche. "Damn them!" she said, with intense anger. "This is a peaceful place. Now the Church wants to start a war so they can burn innocent Perfecti."

Blanche paused, in quiet reflection. "I've never completely agreed with the Cathar belief that the world is of Satan. I can't imagine someone as evil as Satan creating this much love and beauty. But sometimes I wonder."

Pierre grinned.

Blanche had a sense of resignation in her tone. "I will go see the Count of Toulouse—Raymond VI. I will tell him your thoughts and the predicament that is approaching. I can't imagine him standing down. He will protect the Perfecti with his very life."

"He is a loyal supporter, and our most important," Pierre agreed. "Without his army, we are lost."

Blanche nodded. "I fear that a war is coming, and many people are going to die."

* * * * *

The next day, Joanna, Blanche's fourteen-year-old daughter, found Pierre walking in the castle's garden. Ever since Joanna was five, she had sought out Pierre and asked him questions about God and the Perfecti. Her brother, Jean, had never showed a keen interest. But she was curious about this religious man who lived with them and prayed at the dinner table.

"Pierre," Joanna said, running up to him, "what were you talking about at dinner last night? What is a Papal Bull?"

Pierre hesitated. He wasn't sure if he should tell her the truth. "Joanna, I suppose you are old enough to know…"

Joanna heard Pierre's tone of gravity, and she pleaded with him to explain. "Know what, Perfecti Pierre?"

"Please sit," Pierre said, pointing to a stone bench that provided a view of the town.

This was Pierre's favorite spot, the place where he loved to come. The view was spectacular, and the garden was beautiful and tranquil. The castle was high up on a hill, above the town of Laurac, which was nestled below in the valley. The rolling hills of the valley were majestic to view.

The garden was more than just plants and flowers, although they were lushly abundant. There was also a large, clear area of luscious green grass. The grass ran down, away from the castle and toward the town, sloping steadily. At the bottom of the slope was a thick, ten-foot tall stone wall that completely encircled the castle. The wall was so far away, and so low in the horizon, that it did not block the beautiful view of the valley at all.

Pierre sat next to Joanna. Behind them, the castle loomed. It was at least thirty feet tall and two hundred feet wide, and looked even larger because it was perched on a high hill. It was the most imposing castle in Laurac, but no bigger in size than the dozens of others that dotted Languedoc.

"As you are aware, there is a Catholic Church in Laurac."

Joanna nodded, attentively listening.

"That church comes from another country, Italy, which is a few days ride from here by horse. In Italy, they have a church leader called the Pope, and this Pope does not like Cathars. In fact, he dislikes us so much that he has had many Perfecti killed in other countries."

"Killed? What do you mean?" Joanna asked, bewildered. She could not imagine such a thing.

"Burned at the stake. The Catholics and the Gnostics have been competing for the hearts and minds of the people ever since Jesus died on the cross. Soon after the Council of Nicaea in 325 AD, where the New Testament was compiled and the modern Catholic Church came into existence, all of the Gnostics were labeled as heretics. This began the purging and burning of heretics by the Catholic Church. And it continues today throughout Europe."

"Perfecti Pierre, how can they do that?" she asked, incredulous.

"They are very powerful, except here in Languedoc, where the nobles protect us. The Catholic Church believes that only their beliefs are correct, and that it is their duty to God to eliminate all blasphemy from the face of the earth. They have labeled us as heretics, which is just another way of saying that we are blasphemers."

"I don't understand. It's all so confusing," Joanna said, flustered. She was trying to figure out how these strange religious fanatics—who murdered people in the name of God—had managed to affect her life.

Pierre smiled. "Indeed, it is confusing. Let me try to explain. The Catholics believe that our ideas about Mary Magdalene and Jesus are wrong. For instance, they don't believe that Jesus was ever married, or even that Mary Magdalene and her child came to France. Therefore, they don't believe that Mary Magdalene wrote a Gospel here in France, the one that we have been studying since 30 AD. In fact, they are saying that most of our beliefs are blasphemous."

"That is insane!" Joanna exclaimed. "Our beliefs came from Mary Magdalene, which she learned from Jesus. How can they just proclaim that our beliefs are wrong?"

Pierre smiled. "You are right, Joanna. Our beliefs are as solid as the ground we walk upon. We are the *true* descendants."

Joanna calmed down. "I thought so."

She hesitated for a couple of minutes, mulling all of this over.

"Which of our beliefs are so wrong that they would want to kill us?" she finally asked, more intrigued than she had previously been in her life. "They must think that we are evil. But where could they get such an idea?"

Pierre hesitated, unsure about how much information to reveal. "The Catholics do not recognize that they are one with God. They perceive separation between themselves and God. Conversely, we believe that our soul connects us with God. This is considered heresy by the Catholics. We believe that our spirit—our soul—is divine, and thus we are divine. This makes us one with God, and it is only delusion to believe otherwise. Conversely, the Catholics not only don't believe this, but instead believe that our soul can only be saved by the Catholic Church."

"You mean," Joanna interrupted, "I have to be a Catholic or else I can't go to God's Kingdom?"

Pierre nodded, and waited to see how Joanna would reply.

"That is utter nonsense. Mary Magdalene wasn't a Catholic. They must be using fear to make people become Catholic. It's a message of come to church or else. That is not the loving God of which Mary Magdalene spoke. Every soul is guaranteed a place in God's Kingdom. We have to be, if we are God's children. Is there no greater love than the love of a parent for their child?"

Pierre smiled. "I couldn't have said it better myself."

"Where on earth do they think our soul comes from?" Joanna asked, now angry. "Do they think it is created at birth?"

Pierre nodded.

Joanna shook her head. "Oh, this is ridiculous. They don't have a clue, do they Perfecti?"

Pierre shook his head. "No, they are misguided. After Jesus' death, the early Christians were split into two groups: the Gnostics of which Mary Magdalene was a part; and the Catholics, of which the Apostle Peter was the head. The Cathars descended from Mary Magdalene, and are now the last of the Gnostics. The Catholic Church evolved out of Peter's group.

"The Catholics are a lot like the Old Testament," continued Pierre. "They are God fearing. They fear that if they do not live a certain way, such as being a proper Catholic, then God will not save their soul. The Gnostics are God loving. They have no fear of God, because they *know* that God loves them. But more than that, they *know* that their soul connects them to God, making them *one* with God."

Joanna was slow to reply. "I can see why the Catholics are so mad at us. You carry the New Testament—the same Bible that they carry—when you walk among the people preaching. Yet you preach from a completely different perspective. You talk of the God that loves us all. You talk of a God that you personally know, and there is no fear in your words."

Pierre smiled. "You're a prodigy, Joanna, just like your mother. Yes, you're exactly right. Since the Catholics don't understand the soul's direct connection with God, they live by faith. We, on the other hand, live by knowledge. We *know* we're connected to God."

Joanna nodded in agreement. "And this difference is enough for them to want to kill all of the Perfecti?"

Pierre nodded. "Sadly, yes. I think that it is coming soon. I am getting old, but you will witness it one day. Very likely, you will witness the end of the Cathars."

Joanna was saddened. "That is so hard to believe. We are the true descendants, not them. There was no one closer to Jesus or who understood him better than Mary Magdalene. She was the Apostle of the Apostles. How could God let Perfecti be killed for following her?"

"Free will and Satan," Pierre replied, and then smiled. "But that is a discussion for another day. Now, go have fun. It's a beautiful day."

Joanna smiled. "Thank you, Perfecti."

* * * * *

Shortly after the Bull was announced, Cistercian monks began moving into the numerous villages and towns in Languedoc. It was their job to implement the Bull. They also preached and gave sermons, converting people to Catholicism. There were a few debates between the Cistercians and the Perfecti, but those generally occurred in the presence of nobles or large crowds, where the Perfecti felt secure.

The Cistercians had little impact in the region. They did convert many to Catholicism, but they were powerless to implement the Bull without the nobles' support. The only thing Pope Innocent III achieved was replacing several of the Catholic bishops who supported the Cathars with Cistercians. This provided better information gathering, but still left the Pope powerless to persecute the Cathars.

Pope Innocent III was irritated. He wanted to attack heresy in Languedoc, but he was still being stymied. This stalemate lasted until 1209. Finally, French King Phillip Augustus gave his tacit approval for the Pope to invade Languedoc. Finally, the Pope had his chance to eliminate the heretics.

CHAPTER SEVEN

The Albigensian Crusade Begins

In the summer of 1209, the Pope assembled an army of 30,000 men. Most of them were mercenaries who had been paid for only forty days. There were no French Royal Troops, nor any Knights Templar present—only soldiers who would serve anyone for the right price.

After they crossed the Alps into Languedoc, they stopped within sight of Béziers, a town of 10,000 people. Arnaud Amaury, who was in charge, sent a delegation into the town to retrieve a list of heretics. The terms were simple, stark and unequivocal. Unless the town surrendered all of their heretics, immediately, the army would attack.

Showing loyalty for their beloved Perfecti, the people of Béziers refused. And when the delegation returned empty handed, Amaury was incensed. "Kill them all," he roared angrily. "God will know his own."[27]

The ragtag army attacked with abandon. The entire city was plundered. Nearly everyone was killed, including the women and children. Any survivors were lucky to escape Amaury's wrath.

* * * * *

27 There is a general agreement among historians that those were his actual words. If you Google that phrase you will find several references.

When Blanche heard the news of Béziers, she immediately went to see Pierre. He was now frail and in his final years.

She sat down gently beside his bed and waited patiently for Pierre to open his eyes. When he did, she spoke softly.

"Pierre, the war has started," she said. "The Pope has unleashed a crusade against the Cathars. It is being called the Albigensian Crusade, and he has finally sent an army to Languedoc.

"A few days ago, they attacked Béziers," she continued, "and they plundered the town, killing nearly everyone. Then, two days ago, Narbonne surrendered to terms. Twenty-seven Perfecti were burned at the stake."

Pierre was wide awake now, startled by the latest news. He coughed and sat up higher in his bed. "What were the terms?" he asked, in a low trembling voice, the pain in his body evident.

"A list of heretics," Blanche replied, without emotion. "It is just as you have always said. They have come to kill the Perfecti."

Pierre nodded, his eyes revealing the little vitality he had left. "How big is their army? Are there any Royal Troops?"

"It was reported to be an army of mercenaries, quite big in size, into the tens of thousands," Blanche said tensely, hoping that Pierre could give her counsel.

Pierre answered her desire immediately. "Send Joanna to Montségur for protection," he replied. "Tell her to stay until the war is over. She would be safe here for now, but it will be one less thing for you to worry about."

He coughed again, and then went on. "Also, send someone to inform the Count of Toulouse to prepare his army. Ask the Count to confirm that King Phillip Augustus is not involved. If the King joins the Pope, then we have no defense against such a large army; the nobles would have to accept terms. Hopefully, the papal mercenaries have merely been paid for forty days, and then most will go home."

Pierre coughed once more. "I have a feeling this is going to be a long war."

Blanche was highly distressed. She closed her eyes and rubbed her forehead. She had known this day was coming, but she still didn't like it. Joanna, her twenty-three-year-old daughter, had become a Perfecti and was now being threatened. Blanche wasn't even sure that she could protect her. There were many, many Perfecti that she knew, and all of their lives were hanging precariously now by a tenuous thread.

"I will go see Raymond VI in Toulouse," Blanche finally replied. "In fact, I will go today. Joanna will go to Montségur. Should we evacuate the other Perfecti to Foix or Toulouse?"

Pierre shook his head. "No, there will be time for that later. The papal army will go town to town. They won't arrive here for months. And once they do, we can easily outmaneuver them here in Lauragaise, with the nobles' support. There are over a thousand nobles in Languedoc—and many of them live in Lauragaise. It won't be easy for the Crusaders when they come west. As long as the nobles resist, the Pope will have a hard time removing the Cathars."

Blanche knew the question she wanted to ask, but she hesitated, unsure if she wanted to hear the answer. "Pierre, what do you think will be the outcome?"

Pierre looked at Blanche, vitality still in his eyes. "I don't think the Catholics will give up until the Cathars are completely exterminated," he said, matter-of-factly. "However, this war could have many turns, and could last a long time."

He sounded like a statesman instead of a Perfecti now, as he analyzed the situation further.

"The Pope is trying to capture a very wealthy region that has a lot of resistance. The nobles have their own armies, and are quite determined. As long as the King does not intervene, it will take years and years to resolve. As I have always said....

As long as the nobles support us, we will remain. But once they turn their backs, we are finished."

"Pierre, I will never turn my back," Blanche said firmly.

"Not you, Countess," he smiled. "The three Counts who control Languedoc: Peter II, the King of Aragon; Raymond VI, the Count of Toulouse; and, Roger-Raymond Trencavel, the Count of Béziers."

"When I see Raymond VI today, I will tell him your thoughts."

Pierre nodded and forced a weak grin. His health was clearly failing him.

Blanche arose, and left the room.

As soon as she was gone, the grin left his face and was replaced by deep concern. This was the reason he had fought death and had clung to life. He wanted to be here for Blanche, one last time, when the final persecution started.

Now, realizing how long the war would likely last, he recognized that he could not remain with her until the very end. He resigned himself to his fate, and he no longer felt any need to stay. Later that night, he passed over.

* * * * *

As Blanche began her short journey to Toulouse, the papal army was laying siege to the walled fortress at Carcassonne. This was the third stop for the Albigensian Crusade. Carcassonne was the largest town in Languedoc, with a population nearing twenty thousand.

A day earlier, a Crusade delegation had arrived in Carcassonne with terms. The Count of the region, Raymond-Rogers Trencavel, was given forty-eight hours to provide a list of heretics, along with their locations. Two days later, the delegation returned, triumphant, with a list of forty-one Perfecti.

Arnaud Amaury mounted his horse and led the army into town, with the Papal flag leading the way. When they arrived, the town leaders were waiting. Amaury dismounted in his colorful uniform and approached the town leaders.

"The heretics had better be easy to find," Amaury said menacingly. "If there are any problems, we will go door to door searching. And a few homes might just burn by accident."

The leaders were quiet. It was obvious that Amaury was totally consumed by his mission. He was not someone with whom to have a rational conversation.

"We need ten men who can ride and help us find the heretics." Amaury shouted out to the town leaders. "Hurry up and choose! We are ready to begin!"

He then moved on to the next order of business. Amaury ordered burning spires to be built in the town center while his men were searching. "Get plenty of wood, there is a lot of burning to be done!"

A short while later, Amaury returned with five hundred men, only a fraction of his total army. The ten volunteers stood in front of the townspeople. Amaury ordered ten of his men off their horses, and they were replaced by the volunteers.

Before riding off in search of the heretics, Amaury yelled at the men building the spires, "Work fast! When we return, I expect there to be more than one spire ready." It was more of a threat than an order.

"The first name?" Amaury roared out to his soldiers.

One of Amaury's lieutenants, riding next to him, held the list in his hand. He yelled out the name and location.

"Which direction?" Amaury asked the volunteers.

They pointed north. Off they rode.

Soon a heretic's house was invaded, and out he came with hands bound, wearing the ubiquitous brown robe.

"Take him back to town and burn him!" Amaury shouted ruthlessly.

One of the mercenaries dismounted, and the Perfecti was thrown onto his horse for transport. The Perfecti made no struggle, nor voiced any complaint, as several of the mercenaries escorted him back into town.

Once they arrived at the town center, the soldiers bound the Perfecti to a spire and immediately lit it on fire. It was a foul and ghoulish death. There were no last words, nor any trace of justice.

These were mercenaries who had simply come to kill for money. They were like Nazis in their rigid attention to protocol—like robots who were just following orders, and they showed no remorse.

Once the fire had begun, the mercenaries re-mounted their horses and hurried back to the chase. The townspeople watched in horror as the flames engulfed one of their revered Perfecti.

* * * * *

Blanche's trip to Toulouse required only a couple of hours by horse. She traveled with several of her knights, not so much for protection, but for prestige and decorum.

Raymond VI was a close friend of Blanche's, and the wealthiest and most powerful man in Languedoc. The number of nobles with large castles under his domain numbered into the dozens. Many of these castles were fortresses in their own right, as large as his own.

His lands included a large section of southern France: all of the Lauragaise region—the heartland of the Cathars; the wealthy Agenais region to the north; and part of west Languedoc, including the town of Avignon.

Toulouse was one of the most fortified large towns in all of Languedoc. When the gates were closed, it was nearly impossible to penetrate. As Blanche approached Toulouse, she saw a town of ten thousand people that was protected like a fortress. There were large, twenty-foot walls on all four sides of the town. In front of these walls were trenches for further protection.

Château Narbonnais—Raymond VI's castle—was located outside of Toulouse's walls, but nearly adjacent. It was a round fortress, with its own steep walls. In addition to the walls, a moat provided even more resistance. As the Crusaders would come to learn, moats and walls were pervasive in Languedoc.

The castle drawbridge was already lowered, so Blanche crossed the moat swiftly as two of Raymond's hired mercenaries waved her across. Raymond had the largest mercenary army in Languedoc. It numbered into the hundreds, but he could reinforce it into the thousands, if necessary.

As Blanche dismounted her horse, Antoine was there to greet her, and his bright blue tunic revealed his importance at the castle. Antoine was Raymond's young advisor and first lieutenant. He was a knight of the highest caliber.

"Antoine, how nice to see you," Blanche said, holding out her hand.

Antoine kneeled on one knee and kissed her hand. "Countess, always a pleasure. This way, my Lady. Raymond is waiting."

Blanche was dressed in a beautiful white gown that had no place on the back of a horse. But it felt perfectly comfortable to her. She had been riding since she was a girl and enjoyed traveling in Lauragaise, often to visit her numerous friends.

Antoine escorted Blanche through the stone castle to Raymond's study, where he had been reading.

"Blanche," Raymond said with a smile, walking up to greet her, "it's so good to see you again."

Raymond VI was dressed in his dramatic Count regalia, sporting a colorful red tunic and baggy striped pants. If he walked among the people, there would be no doubt that he was an important noble.

She held out her hand and he kissed it.

"What brings you to Toulouse?"

Blanche sat back in a huge comfortable chair, and took a deep breath before broaching the gruesome topic at hand. "The Pope has begun a crusade against the Cathars," she began.

Raymond sat across from her in his large chair, which dominated the room. The room was immense, with a very tall ceiling and two fireplaces. It was entirely made of stone with thick carpets throughout the floor. There were no windows, which kept the room pungent and relatively dark, even with a large chandelier of candles. The disordered ancient books and scrolls on one of the walls revealed that this is where Raymond spent much of his time.

"I know," Raymond replied. "They're in Carcassonne today, burning Perfecti."

Blanche shook her head in anguish. "Has there been any resistance?"

"No, although Béziers refused their terms. Those idiots! There were only two dozen Perfecti in Béziers. I would say that only perhaps half of the people of Béziers even supported the Cathars. Why did they die for something they didn't believe in?"

Blanche hesitated. She wished that she had asked Pierre about Béziers before she had left. "Perhaps, they didn't expect a pillage. Like you said, everyone knows that there aren't that many Perfecti in Béziers."

Raymond VI shook his head in disgust at the loss of human lives. "No, I think they just hate Catholics. Languedoc has never been a Catholic bastion. Even most of those who don't support the Cathars are not Catholic. So I think they just took a stand against the Catholic Church."

Blanche nodded at the possibility. However, it was already too late for Béziers, so she quickly decided to move on. "Pierre said that the Cathars would exist as long as they had the support of the nobles. Do you agree?"

Raymond VI grinned. "He is one of the wisest men in Languedoc, and yes, he is correct. As long as I am alive, the Cathars will exist, and when my son, Raymond VII is old enough, he will carry on that mission. We have strength in Languedoc. The Crusaders will not defeat us."

"Pierre is not worried about them. It's the French Royal Army that concerns him. The King."

Raymond raised his eyebrows. "Why? King Phillip will never invade Languedoc. These are my lands. There is nothing to worry about."

Blanche did not offer a reply, and simply stared down at her hands, nervously. But she knew Pierre too well. She knew that if he feared the Royal Army, then one day it would surely come.

"Are we going to agree to terms here in Lauragaise?" she asked.

Raymond VI hesitated. "Well, I can defend Toulouse, but not all of Lauragaise. Laurac is likely threatened. You should evacuate the Perfecti and send them here for safekeeping."

Raymond could see the worry on the face of the Countess, so he sought to reassure her once and for all. "There will be no terms in Toulouse," he thundered. "We are prepared for any attack."

Blanche still looked dejected, as she questioned him meekly. "You can protect the Cathars only in Toulouse?"

"Countess, today, yes—although that could change. If the Crusader army becomes smaller, then I may attack. It is hard to say, so I cannot promise any more than this."

"And what about the other regions of Languedoc?" she asked. "Do you think there will be any resistance?"

Raymond hesitated, not sure how much to divulge. "The region of Albige to the east is protected by Roger-Raymond Trencavel. The region of Foix to the south is protected by Peter II of Aragon. Also, the Count of Comminges will defend the

Comminges region to the southwest. It is not going to be easy for the Crusaders."

Suddenly Blanche brightened and grinned, inspired by his positive attitude. "Thank you, Raymond. That is all I came for. If you need anything, let me know." She arose.

"It is always a pleasure, Blanche. Tell Pierre hello and to keep in touch."

"His days are short," Blanche said, with obvious emotion creeping into her voice. She wasn't quite ready to let go of Pierre just yet.

"I know. But be strong, Blanche. He's been telling us about this war for years, even before the Catholics themselves knew they were coming."

"There is so much at stake," Blanche replied, ready to depart.

Raymond VI nodded solemnly, and Blanche turned and left.

Upon her arrival home, Blanche made the sad discovery that Pierre had died quietly in his sleep the night before. She knew that she would miss his counsel and friendship. But she was also glad that he had finally gone home to find peace.

* * * * *

Joanna made it to Montségur and hiked to the walled entrance. The hike was somewhat challenging, even for a young person of her age. She had long straight blonde hair and was a beauty like her mother. Her smile could make anyone feel better for being in her presence.

This was the most imposing fortress in Languedoc. Built at the top of a steep hill, it appeared impenetrable from the valley floor. Any attacker would have the difficult task of hiking a tremendously steep hill, and then penetrating the thirty-foot walls at the very top.

When Joanna arrived at the entrance she smiled at the symbols on the main gates. The left gate had a large circle with an equidistant cross in the middle carved into the wood. The right gate had a large pentagram carved into it. She knew that she was at the right place, as these were a sacred Cathar symbols. The circle represented eternal life and the cross equality among people. The pentagram represented purity and perfection—the goal of every Cathar.

She was met at the gates by several Perfecti, easily recognizable in their matching brown robes. They had been expecting her, and now made her feel most welcome. They had moved to this place in 1204, soon after it was completed. They used it as a monastery, and often traveled throughout Languedoc on missionary work. Now that the crusade had begun, it would be their base of operations.

Inside the tall gates, the fortress was enclosed by thick tall stone walls. It was an imposing place, not the usual surroundings for a monastery. It was relatively empty for such a large fortress. Joanna only saw two other people, besides the Perfecti.

"Come inside," one of the Perfecti said, "we will find you a room of your own and give you a tour."

Joanna smiled. "That would be nice."

They walked across the large empty courtyard and entered the fortress. One of the Perfecti opened a wooden door and led Joanna down a long stone hallway to the great room. It, too, was empty, except for a fire in one of the large fireplaces, which were situated at each end of the room. Long rectangular tables were aligned in two rows, enough to seat more than a hundred people.

"Where are all the people for such a large place?" Joanna asked.

"We had only six Perfecti until you arrived. Now we have seven. We also have three servants for cooking and cleaning. That will all change, now that a crusade has begun. You are the first, but there will likely be a stream of Perfecti arriving soon."

They walked through the great room and down another stone hallway to the bedrooms.

"You can choose whatever room you like. There are many available," said one of the Perfecti.

Joanna poked her head into several of the rooms and picked one. "This one is fine. The bed looks soft."

She walked into her new room and placed her bag on the bed.

"Okay, then we'll be back later to show you around."

Joanna nodded, and they were gone. She decided to create a small altar to create a sense of sacredness in her room. There was a shelf that would serve that purpose. She removed her valuable scrolls that Pierre had given her from her bag, along with the Book of Love, and placed them on the altar. Then she removed a small white dove made out of ivory, along with a silver chalice. She placed these next to the scrolls on the shelf. Then she removed some herbs from her bag and placed them on the shelf. Lastly, she removed some small stones and crystals which were added to the altar.

Several minutes later, Gilbert de Castres, a fellow Perfecti and friend of Joanna's, came to see her. He walked in with a welcoming smile. "Hello, Joanna, it is good to see you. What brings you to Montségur?"

Joanna forced a smile, thinking about the unfortunate event that had brought her here. "Hello, Gilbert. Please sit."

Gilbert sat in the only available chair. Joanna remained sitting on her bed. He was only a few years older than Joanna. He had dark hair and an unshaven face. He was handsome and a very likable person.

"My mother sent me to live here," Joanna began, sadly, "because a war has begun." Fear began to creep into her tone as she thought about recent events. "The Pope has sent a crusading army to destroy all of the Cathars in Languedoc. Béziers has already been pillaged, and everyone was killed. Carcassonne surrendered, and many Perfecti were burned at the stake there."

Gilbert nodded solemnly. "Yes, we have been informed. Joanna, it is much too soon to give up hope. Languedoc is very big, and you know that the nobles support us. Besides, we are very safe here. I don't think that we should be worried just yet. Let's wait and see what happens."

"I'm scared," Joanna replied anxiously. "Pierre told me when I was a young girl that this day would come. He said that Gnostics have been persecuted for centuries by the Catholics. He said they would persecute us, too."

"Yeah, I remember Perfecti Pierre. He used to call the Catholics the Anti-Christ church, because of their butchery. Yes, they've been burning Gnostics for centuries. This is nothing new to us. They believe that they are doing their duty to God."

"Isn't it ironic, Gilbert? We would never lift a hand against the Catholics. Yet we are the ones who are persecuted. We have love in our hearts for them, yet they have wrath and condemnation in their hearts for us. Where did such a religion come from?"

"From a false beginning," Gilbert replied. "They rejected the *nous* as a path to God, the most important message of Jesus. Instead, they built a religion based on a judgmental God, a God of expectations. A God that expects everyone to be Catholic. Those who are not Catholics are to be purged."

"So they are killing us out of duty?" Joanna asked. "They are killing us because they believe that their God expects them to?"

Gilbert nodded. "Yes. They believe that they are expected to eliminate heretics. They believe it is their duty as Catholics."

Joanna shook her head. "They are murderers, no better than the barbarians of the dark ages!"

Gilbert nodded. "Yes. Only this time they hide behind papal vestments and the so-called legitimacy of Papal Bulls."

"And their gilded cathedrals," Joanna added.

CHAPTER EIGHT

The Perfecti Women's Home

Antoine rode across the moat and entered Château Narbonnais, with several fellow knights following. He dismounted his horse, and a servant grabbed the horse's reigns and took possession. Antoine quickly walked to the castle to find the Count.

He could tell by the smell of the fireplace that the Count was in his study. This was the first place he looked, as the Count was a voracious reader and spent most of his time there. He entered the room and stood at attention wearing his knightly attire, albeit without any armor.

Raymond VI put down the scroll he was reading and addressed Antoine. "Yes, Antoine?"

"My Lord, Simon de Montfort is now in charge of the crusade. He is a baron from the north. Perhaps you have heard of him?"

Raymond nodded. "He is a worthy opponent. What has Roger-Raymond Trencavel been doing?"

"He has been arrested and placed in his own dungeon in Carcassonne. All of the Trencavel lands were confiscated by the Crusaders."

Raymond rose from his chair and walked toward the fireplace, unable to sit still. "They are audacious," he said calmly, with no hint of emotion. "Just like that, all of his lands taken? This new Pope is certainly determined."

Raymond stopped pacing and turned to Antoine, who was still standing at attention across the room. "What else?"

"Montfort was voted Count of Carcassonne and Béziers. However, no land was given to him. That can only be done by the Pope, in writing."

In the spring of 1214, Pope Innocent III sent Cardinal Peter of Benevento to Carcassonne to negotiate a

settlement of Languedoc.

"And the King!" Raymond roared angrily. He was losing his patience with the events of the day. "We are vassals of the French Monarchy. The Pope can't just ignore that fact!"

"Yes, my Lord," Antoine replied. "Also, the army has been reduced in size. It is now less than a thousand men, with only three hundred horses."

Raymond was stunned. "That is all? They can't come to Toulouse with that army! And the nobles in the Carcassonne region will surely resist such a small army."

"Perhaps the Pope is not so wealthy?" Antoine said. "Maybe the Crusades to the holy lands have emptied their treasury."

Raymond contemplated. "Maybe. But I don't think the King is going to help him with more gold. And with such a small army, I don't know what the Pope is thinking."

"Time will tell, my Lord."

Raymond dismissed Antoine, and calculated his situation.

* * * * *

A few months later, Blanche went to Montségur to see Joanna. When she arrived—after the steep hike—she was surprised to find nearly fifty Perfecti in the courtyard. After the fall of Béziers, Narbonne, and Carcassonne, many Perfecti had come here for safety.

A Perfecti met Blanche at the gates and escorted her to Joanna's room. When Blanche entered the room, Joanna rose immediately and embraced her mother.

"Mother! It is so good to see you."

Like the rest of Montségur, Joanna's room had only basic furnishings. There were no framed paintings or ornate decorations anywhere to be found at the fortress. It was built to protect the Cathars, and there was nothing ostentatious. Joanna had a straw bed, a candle lamp, a trunk for her clothes, and two wooden chairs. It was not much different than the other rooms, other than the altar that she had made on her single shelf. She had no heating, and in the winter it was quite cold.

The Countess was wearing one of her colorful gowns and looked conspicuously out of place. Joanna, of course, wore her brown robe.

"Sit, Mother. You must be tired from that long hike."

Blanche found a seat. "It was not easy for this old body."

"Mother, you are only forty-four. That is not old."

Blanche smiled. "I would rather be your age."

"Would you like something to eat?"

"Water would be nice," Blanche replied.

"Okay, let me get you some, and I want to find Gilbert. He would like to hear what you have to say. I'll be right back."

Joanna left Blanche alone, and darted out of the room. Shortly after, she returned with a wooden cup of water and Gilbert at her side. She handed the cup to a seated Blanche.

"Mother, do you remember Gilbert?"

Blanche held out her hand, "Of course! Hello, Perfecti."

Gilbert knelt on one knee and kissed her hand. "Countess."

Joanna sat on her bed, and left the remaining chair for Gilbert. "What news do you bring, Mother?"

In the serious tone of a Countess, Blanche said, "The crusade is progressing in the Carcassonne region. Most of the towns and villages are agreeing to terms and turning over their Perfecti, who have been killed by being burned at the stake. The crusading army has been reduced in size, and they are making slow progress. Also, there has been some resistance from the nobles, but nothing to stop the Crusaders."

"Where has the resistance come from?" Gilbert asked.

"The fortresses of Minerve, Termes, and Cabaret. They only have small mercenary armies, nothing of the size that Roger-Raymond Trencavel had before he was arrested."

Gilbert nodded and then asked more questions. "What about the Counts of Foix, Comminges, and Toulouse? Why have they not come to the defense of the Carcassonne region?"

"It's not their land," Blanche replied. "At this time, they are making preparations to defend their own lands."

"And what about Laurac?" Joanna asked. "Are the Crusaders going there next?"

Blanche shook her head. "No, Raymond said that the Crusader army isn't big enough to invade the Lauragaise. I think we are safe for now."

"Then can I come home for a couple of days?" Joanna pleaded. "I want to visit the Perfecti Women's Home! I need to see my girls!"

Blanche hesitated. "If you stay for only a couple of days, I'll agree to it."

Joanna smiled joyously. "Thank you, Mother. It will feel good to be home and sleep in my own bed."

"I will accompany her," Gilbert said. "She will be safe."

Blanche smiled. "You are always welcome to stay at the castle, Gilbert."

"Thank you, Countess."

* * * * *

A couple of days later, Gilbert and Joanna walked to Laurac. Their first stop was the Perfecti Women's Home. It was a nondescript wooden home near the middle of town. The locals knew who lived there, but the women Perfecti and those in training rarely interacted with the local population.

In the past, women Perfecti had often preached in public, but that was no longer the custom. Nearly all debates between the Cistercian monks and Perfecti were between men. It was not forbidden for women Perfecti to preach publicly, it was just uncommon.

The Perfecti women did occasionally pray publicly for individuals who made public requests. It was not uncommon to see a man prostrated on the ground in front of a female Perfecti—pleading for forgiveness, God's blessing, or the *consolamentum.* And when women Perfecti did interact with the local population for spiritual reasons, they were accepted the same as men.

Besides Joanna's girls, there were also women in training at the home. But Joanna was young, light of spirit, and preferred to teach only her teenaged girls. It was her project.

Since this was like her second home, Joanna opened the front door without knocking. "Hello, girls," she called out, as she entered.

The women's home was big with ten bedrooms and several large rooms where people could congregate. The front room, where Joanna and Gilbert had entered, had a large fireplace and many chairs and small tables. There was enough space for at least twenty people. In the winter time, they could all gather here to stay warm. Over the fireplace was an altar that included a pentagram, a white dove, several carved roses, and a silver chalice. On one of the walls was a framed picture of Mary Magdalene. It was the only picture in the house.

The girls were all quite excited to see her, after her long absence, and immediately followed her to the teaching room.

Joanna waved briefly, as a greeting to her fellow teachers, but she did not introduce her friend Gilbert, knowing that these women Perfecti rarely interacted with men.

Joanna smiled joyfully, as she and Gilbert and the girls all found a place to sit in the large room in the back of the house. "It is wonderful to be back and see all of your faces!"

The girls all smiled back at her, but they were not as joyous.

"Perfecti Joanna, we are afraid. A crusade has started. A crusade to kill Perfecti!"

Joanna nodded. "I know. That is why I have not visited in such a long time. I have been at Montségur, safely behind the walls."

"Are we going to die?" one of the girls asked, terrified.

Joanna closed her eyes for a moment and silently prayed. Then she slowly looked around at all of their worried faces. "I know that you are all young and that my words may not soothe you, but I am here to help you understand. Will you be patient with me today and try?"

The girls all nodded.

"Okay. Now, what have I taught you about your soul?"

Joanna waited for someone to reply.

"That it is divine and connected to God," someone replied.

Joanna smiled. "Yes. And what else?"

"That it is eternal," another girl said.

"Yes! Exactly! That is what you must understand. Our body is not the soul's home. Our soul resides in God's Kingdom, which is our true home. Jesus told this to Mary Magdalene after the resurrection. He arose as spirit! When she saw him, she saw his soul, which resides in God's Kingdom. This is why he told her not to touch him. The home of our eternal soul is God's Kingdom."

"Are you saying, Perfecti Joanna, that there is no such thing as death? That our soul is always alive in God's Kingdom?"

Joanna nodded. "Yes. That is Mary Magdalene's message, and I believe it."

"Does everyone return to God's Kingdom?" someone asked.

"Yes, eventually we all do. Those who are not yet ready to live in God's Kingdom must reincarnate back here. They must be reborn into another body and live again. And those who come back to this world must encounter Satan again. This world of matter is Satan's. That is why there is death and destruction.

"God's Kingdom is of spirit, and matter does not exist there. It is a place of perfection where only good is found. Here, in the land of Satan, the land of matter, we have all kinds of temptations and evil. It is quite the opposite of God's Kingdom."

"Why would we even come here, Perfecti Joanna?" another girl asked. "If our soul does not live here, then why would we come?"

Joanna smiled. "Excellent question. We come here of our own free will. This is something that was taught to me by my teacher, Perfecti Pierre, who has passed on and returned to God's Kingdom. He told me all about free will and why we would choose to come here.

"Every soul is a part of God and has the potential to evolve and become more like God. We literally have infinite potential. However, achieving that potential requires experiences and lessons. This is why we come and expose ourselves to Satan.

"For instance, we come here so that we can *know* the depths of God's love and God's compassion. For, until you experience love's opposite—hate—and compassion's opposite—indifference—you cannot truly *know*. These are only two examples of lessons that can be learned. There are many, many others. What Pierre taught me was that our soul becomes more evolved, more aware, once it has experienced Satan."

One girl looked confused and asked, "Why would God do that? Why would God expose us to evil? You would think there would be a better way to learn."

"God doesn't," Joanna replied. "We choose to come. It is our choice."

"I wouldn't come! I would stay there with God in the Kingdom!" she replied.

Joanna smiled. "That is what I told Pierre, too. He said that it can be boring in God's Kingdom with all that perfection and love. After meeting other souls who have incarnated and experienced Satan, we get curious about their experiences.

"Not only that, but we can watch other souls who are currently incarnated. Thus, even if we aren't incarnated, we can come down here and see what is happening. Pierre said that we can even choose which life to live, if we decide to incarnate."

The same girl looked confused. "In advance? We see the life we are going to live? Will we know everything about it?"

Joanna nodded.

"That sounds interesting," the same girl said. "*Then* you wouldn't be afraid. You would know the outcome!"

Joanna nodded again. "When we are here, it appears like Hell. But when we look at it from God's Kingdom, incarnating looks very intriguing and rewarding."

"Do the Catholics know about this?" a girl asked.

Joanna shook her head. "No, they don't believe in reincarnation."

"Then they must be afraid of death. It must be a big unknown for them," a girl said.

Joanna shook her head. "No, many of them have faith in God's Kingdom. After all, that was a major part of Jesus' message. However, whereas they have faith, we have knowledge."

"But don't they also believe in Hell?" a girl asked. "Some of them must be afraid of going to Hell?"

"Let's not talk about Catholics in a negative manner," Joanna said sternly. "That is just gossip. 'Leave them to their own devices,' is what Pierre used to tell me. Let's remember the vows. A Perfecti is not to condemn. They are our brothers and sisters, too."

"I wasn't judging them, Perfecti Joanna. I'm just trying to understand them better," the girl said.

Joanna hesitated. "Okay. On my next visit, I will tell you more about the differences between the Cathars and the Catholics."

"Can you tell us now about the crusade?" a girl asked.

Joanna nodded. "Well, after our discussion this morning, you should no longer be afraid. If the Crusaders threaten our lives, and they probably will, we should not fear death. The end of this lifetime is simply a destiny, a time to go home, a time to return to God's Kingdom."

"I'm not afraid of dying," a girl said, "but I'm afraid that Languedoc will no longer have any Perfecti."

Joanna sighed. "That is my fear, as well. It is possible for that outcome, because of what Pierre called free will. In the land of matter, the land of Satan, God gave all of humankind free will. God does not interfere. That is why Satan came here to create his mischief.

"Humankind is free to choose how they want to live and how they want to worship God. If humankind, such as the powerful Catholics, decide to eliminate the Cathars, then God will not stand in the way. That is what free will ordains."

"That sounds dreadful," one girl bemoaned.

"That was my reaction, too," Joanna said. "Pierre said that, for there to be peace on earth, humankind has to achieve it on our own. We have to show God our devotion; otherwise Satan will rule.

"That is why we meditate; that is why we take vows to live a pious, ascetic, simple life. As well as a life of compassion, respect, tolerance, and equality. Our mission is to be in alignment with love and to prepare the soul for the return to God's Kingdom. We are setting an example, trying to create peace on earth for the entire world. We can only do this by remaining gentle, peaceful, and pure of heart. This may not prevent the Perfecti from perishing, but it is all we can do.

"There is hope, however," Joanna said. "Pierre told me of a prophecy in The Book of Love written by Mary Magdalene. It states that the Gnostic branch will be eliminated by Peter's Church, but will rise again, in millennia."

"What does that mean, Perfecti Joanna?" a girl asked, intrigued.

"Anyone?" Joanna asked.

A girl raised her hand. "It means that the Cathars are going to be burned at the stake. And that one day, in the far future, they will rise again."

Joanna nodded. "That's correct."

"When is millennia?" someone asked.

"At least a thousand years," Joanna replied.

"So, Perfecti Joanna, you're saying that we are all going to be burned at the stake?"

"That is possible. What you all need to meditate on is that we are not going to die, but we are simply going to go home. We are going back to the Kingdom. Some of you will incarnate again and perhaps experience the end of the Catholic Church and the rise of the Gnostics. The rest of us will remain in God's Kingdom and watch from above."

"So the outcome is a good ending?" one of the girls asked.

Joanna smiled. "Yes. One day there will be peace on earth, and *all* will hold the Gnostic belief of oneness. That we are all connected to one another and with God. Humanity will become one family of God that lives together peacefully and joyfully, all in alignment with love."

CHAPTER NINE

The First Battle—1210

After the shameless plundering of Béziers, nearly a year passed until the first battle between the Crusaders and the resistance. It began on June 3rd, 1210, at the Minerve fortress. It wasn't really a battle – more of a prolonged siege by the Crusaders against members of the resistance, who were trapped behind the walls of the fortress.

Several of Raymond VI's knights had been following the Crusaders at a distance. So, once the siege began, Raymond was kept informed. Minerve was located just fifty miles southeast of Toulouse, near Narbonne on the Mediterranean coastline.

Nearly two months after the siege began, one of Raymond's knights galloped into Château Narbonnais and informed Antoine of the imminent fall of Minerve. Antoine immediately sought Raymond, inside the castle, to inform him of the situation.

Antoine found Raymond reading in his study, as usual. He took two steps into the room and stood at attention.

"Hello, Antoine. I heard a galloping horse cross the moat. Did you receive news from Minerve?"

"Yes, my Lord. Montfort has nearly broken through the front wall. They have built two large trebuchets and have been bombarding it for over a month. They can't hold out much longer. The wall is crumbling."

Raymond winced, and then nodded to acknowledge that he understood. "Tomorrow we will ride to Minerve. I want to see this for myself."

"Lord, how many knights would you like to bring?"

"Just me and you. That way, the Crusaders will not detect us."

Antoine nodded and left the room.

* * * * *

The next day, Raymond and Antoine rode to Minerve. When they arrived, the trebuchets were still heaving heavy, hundred-pound stones a distance of three hundred feet into the front wall, which was the only weakness of the fortress. The remaining three sides were protected by sheer cliffs.

The damage from the continuous bombardment was apparent. The Crusaders kept trying to break through the wall, but they were being repelled by the knights from within. It looked like the battle would be over soon—just as soon as Montfort's army penetrated the wall.

The pair camped nearby, shielded by a large formation of trees. The next morning, Antoine woke up Raymond with the news.

"Lord, it is over. They have surrendered."

Raymond sat up, rubbing his eyes while becoming alert. He could smell the smoke of the bonfire, off in the distance. "Ah, the fire has started," he said. "They are going to burn the Perfecti."

Raymond quickly got dressed and mounted his horse. Arriving at their lookout spot, he could see nearly fifty robed Perfecti being marched to the bonfire. It was a chilling sight. Most of the Perfecti were forcibly thrown into the fire, although there were some who ran and jumped in on their own.

After the burning, the knights who defended the fortress were quickly executed by the Crusaders. The rest of the people in the fortress escaped the sword that day. They were lucky. In the battles to come, many of the towns that resisted would lose all of their citizens to Montfort's fury.

* * * * *

In August 1210, Montfort laid siege to the fortress at Termes, one of the last remaining defenses in the Carcassonne region. It was located twenty miles southwest of Minerve.

The outcome was nearly the same as Minerve. After a month of bombardment by the trebuchets, Raymond de Termes surrendered his fortress to Montfort and the Crusaders.

After Termes fell, Blanche went to visit Raymond. She was not at all confident that he would defend Lauragaise, since he had said as much, and it was becoming apparent that the Crusaders were heading her way.

She mounted her horse, wearing a cloak over an elegant gown, and rode with three of her knights. They arrived a couple of hours later at Château Narbonnais. Antoine met them at the entrance, and escorted the Countess to see Raymond.

Blanche made a stunning picture as she entered Raymond's study without her cloak, revealing a flowing, dark green gown. Her hair was neatly lifted on top of her head. You would never known that she had just ridden twenty miles.

Her longtime friend was wearing a bright red tunic, embroidered with gold, and black pants that ended just below his knees, leaving room for his tall black leather boots. His long, unkempt locks fell down to his shoulders.

Raymond did not get up as she entered. He held out an open hand and directed it towards the chair across from him. "Hello, Blanche, have a seat. Would you like something to drink?"

"No, thank you, Raymond. I won't be staying long," she said, with her best Countess formality, sitting down. "I have come to talk about the crusade. Raymond, the Crusaders and their trebuchets have sacked Raymond de Termes' fortress. All of the Perfecti were burned."

Raymond nodded. "I know, Blanche. At Minerve, as well. I have been following it. My men have been watching."

"Raymond, Termes is one of the largest fortresses in Languedoc. If they can sack Termes, then no one is safe." Blanche spoke logically and without fear. Her voice projected a sense of clear determination and calm analysis.

Raymond nodded. "It is a pity that Raymond de Termes died, along with his strong mercenary army. It is also a pity that his mother and wife were both burned as heretics. As you know, they were both Holy Perfecti."

Blanche had not been informed of their deaths, and her firm resolve slightly faltered. "They were my friends," she said emotionally, holding back her sudden tears. "The Crusaders are killing the holy ones without regard to their sanctity. How can God allow this?"

"Maybe the Cathars are right?" Raymond replied without emotion. "Maybe this is Satan's land. Maybe it is Satan who is killing the Perfecti." It was obvious that the war was starting to wear on him as well, and he was feeling somewhat frustrated.

Blanche wiped her eyes. "Where will the Crusaders go next?"

"I believe it will be Cabaret, Countess. It is the last fortress with a large resistance army in the Carcassonne region. And then ... Montfort may come to the Lauragaise after that, so be prepared."

Blanche had been expecting this warning, but fear was beginning to affect her composure again. "Will you defend us, Raymond?" Blanche asked pleadingly.

"No. I'm sorry, Blanche, but you know that my place is here. I will stay and defend Toulouse from behind the walls."

Blanche shuddered at the thought of oncoming soldiers invading her own back yard. "Our way of life is truly threatened now," she said solemnly.

"Perhaps. Or perhaps not. The end has not yet been determined. Have faith, Blanche. We are all walking towards our destiny. That is all that we can do."

* * * * *

In December, 1210, Joanna and Gilbert returned to Laurac, to visit Blanche and to teach the girls at the Perfecti Women's Home.

Blanche greeted them with a grim warning. "You must only stay a day or two," she said nervously. "Perfecti are not safe in Lauragaise right now."

"Why, mother?" Joanna asked sadly. She was frustrated and wanted to stay for at least a week.

"Pierre-Roger, the Lord of Cabaret, has agreed to terms with the Crusaders. He disbanded his entire army and surrendered his fortress to Montfort. Pierre-Roger was exiled to Provence. His was the last resistance army in the Carcassonne region. So all of Carcassonne is now in the hands of the Crusaders.

"I think that Montfort will most likely come here next," Blanche continued. "And Raymond is not going to defend us."

Gilbert and Joanna knew of the movements of the crusade from the Perfecti who kept arriving at Montségur. However, they had not heard about Cabaret, or realized the dire consequences for Laurac.

"Mother, why isn't Raymond going to defend us?" Joanna asked, alarmed by the news.

"He is going to defend Toulouse from behind its protected walls," Blanche replied gently. "We must each take care of our own first."

"He wants to keep his lands," Gilbert interjected thoughtfully. "As long as he does not attack the Crusaders first, he can always agree to terms. But if he attacks, then he will be labeled as a heretic supporter, and the Crusaders will lay claim to his lands."

"Can the Crusaders really do that to Raymond?" Blanche asked fearfully.

Gilbert nodded. "They did it in Carcassonne, to Raymond-Rogers Trencavel. They arrested him, and he died in irons in his own dungeon. The same thing could happen to Raymond VI."

"But Raymond is one the King's largest vassals," Blanche replied, pleading for a better answer.

"So was Raymond-Rogers."

"Enough of this war talk," Joanna said firmly. She was tired of being afraid. "I want to go see my girls."

Blanche hugged her daughter goodbye. "Joanna, it is no longer safe in Lauragaise. Please be careful."

"Yes, Mother. We will be back for supper."

Blanche smiled, as she bid them farewell. "Tell all the girls hello, and ask if there is anything they need."

"Okay. I will see you tonight."

Gilbert and Joanna walked away in their matching brown robes. They left the castle swiftly, and proceeded to the Perfecti Women's Home in Laurac, which was a long walk down into the valley.

Once they arrived in Laurac, a lady saw them walking through town and prostrated herself at their feet.

"Please pray for me, Perfecti," she pleaded. "Please, forgive my sins."

Joanna began reciting the Lord's Prayer, and then she continued to pray out loud for the woman. "Lord, show mercy for the sins of the flesh and pardon them, for they are not our true self. Lord, show mercy for the false self, which is imprisoned in this body. The flesh is imperfect, but the spirit is perfect. Pardon our imperfections, and bless the perfection of our soul."

"Rise," Joanna told the lady, who was still prostrated.

"You are forgiven," Joanna said, smiling as the lady rose. "Your soul is perfect, without imperfection. The Lord will always forgive the sins of the flesh, which are born of imperfection.

"Know that you and God are one, and that it is your soul that connects you to God. Go in peace, and know that you cannot die, because your soul is eternal. You only have one destiny. And that is to live eternally in heaven, with Jesus and Mary Magdalene, and all of your loved ones."

"Thank you, Perfecti. Thank you," the lady said, with sincere appreciation.

Joanna nodded, and they continued walking towards the town center.

"You are a natural, Joanna," Gilbert said brightly. "You preach from your heart."

"It is what I love to do—share God with others."

As Gilbert and Joanna—a male and a female Perfecti—walked through Laurac, talking to the people, it wasn't that much different from the days of Mary Magdalene, where it had all begun nearly 1200 years earlier.

* * * * *

Soon they reached the Women's home. They entered without knocking, but at first it appeared that the house was empty. Most of the girls were quietly studying in their rooms. Others were cooking in the kitchen, as all of the girls at the home were required to help with various chores.

As Joanna and Gilbert headed toward the back of the house, Joanna found three of her girls seated in the kitchen, where they had been chopping vegetables to make soup.

"Hello girls!" Joanna greeted them, as usual, with a joyous smile. "How nice to see you all again!"

The girls were quickly on their feet, and rushing to hug Joanna.

"Are you going to give us a lesson today?" one of the girls asked.

"Of course. Am I not your teacher?"

"Thank goodness," the same girl replied. "The other Perfecti never tell us the interesting things that you do. They always want us to study scripture and the ancient scrolls."

Joanna smiled. "I'll try to make it interesting."

One of the girls quickly scooped up the vegetables with her hands and put them in a pot on the stove. "We can go now. This will cook for awhile."

Joanna waved to the girls to move into the teaching room. "Let's go begin."

One of the girls raced upstairs to inform the others, and soon everyone had gathered together in the large teaching room.

There were seven teenaged girls in brown robes seated near the front of the room. Joanna suddenly noticed that each girl had adorned her robe in some unique manner. One girl had sewn a lovely small butterfly on her sleeve. Another had sewn her first name on the front in small letters. One had to smile at their youthful creativity.

"The last time I was here," Joanna began, "I promised that I would speak to you about the differences between the Catholics and the Cathars. Is that still what you want to talk about today?"

She quickly scanned the girls faces, and all of the girls nodded.

"Okay, then let's begin," Joanna said. "There is one spectacular difference, and it is the one thing that truly divides us. Without this difference, we would likely be in agreement for most of our beliefs. And that difference involves how we perceive God. We believe that we *are* God, whereas the Catholics believe that they are *separate* from God."

Joanna paused. "Does everyone understand how significant this difference is?"

"Enough to want to kill us?" a girl replied lightly, with a silly grin.

All of the girls laughed.

Joanna nodded sternly. "Yes, it is that significant, but it is not a laughing matter. In fact, this belief determines the foundation of countries. Even more than that, it determines our way of life.

"Also, the Catholics do not believe in reincarnation. They believe that we live one life and then God judges us. We either go to God's Kingdom or to Hell. Furthermore, they believe that the only way to God's Kingdom is through the Catholic Church. In other words, only the Catholics can go to Heaven.

"Now let's continue on," Joanna said in a serious tone, imploring the girls not to make any more silly jokes.

"The Catholics do not search within for God—because they do not believe that God can possibly be found. They think it is our folly to search. Little do they know that this is the gateway to God's Kingdom and to inner peace. Our search is what makes us Gnostics, and what gives us direct knowledge of God.

"As Cathars, our motivation and desire must be to find God. Every day is a new opportunity to be vigilant. We can live with a pure heart, gentle, loving, content, grateful, and not prideful. We renounce hatred, envy, and anger, because they are not in alignment with love. For, God is found through purity, innocence, and a diligent mind."

Joanna scanned the girls. "So how do we come to know God?"

"Through the *nous*," one girl replied. "In her Gospel, Mary Magdalene spoke of the *nous*—our inner consciousness—being directly connected to God's soul."

Joanna nodded. "Exactly. Well spoken," she smiled at the girl and then continued.

"There is only one soul—God's soul—and all consciousness is connected to it. Our souls are like spokes on a wheel, all connected to the hub, or God's soul. The hub is like a base that connects us all. This connection allows God to hear our prayers. It also allows any two souls to communicate on a soul level. You can pray to me at night and my soul will hear you. You can pray to Mary Magdalene and her soul will hear you. You can pray to Jesus and his soul will hear you. All because of our eternal connection to one another."

"You mean the Catholics don't know about the *nous*?" a wide-eyed girl asked, incredulous. She had always believed that it was something everyone could feel.

Joanna slowly shook her head. "No. The Catholics believe that God is separate from us, and that there is no such thing as one 'all-encompassing soul' that connects us all together.

"This is why they think we are heretics," Joanna continued. "They believe that if something is not in the Bible, then it must be heresy."

"But Jesus said that the Kingdom of God is within," another girl said. "And *that's* in the Bible."

Joanna grinned. "Ah, yes. Sounds like the *nous* to me."

Joanna paused, still grinning. "I don't know how the Catholics haven't figured that one out yet. Anyway, our true self is our spirit—the soul—not our body. The body is matter, but the soul is spirit. It is the spirit that gives us life. It is the spirit that connects everything. The consciousness of a plant, an animal, even water and air, are all connected to God. Spirit is consciousness. Spirit is God. This is our true identity.

"The body is nothing without spirit," Joanna continued. "Remove the spirit and the body withers. Therefore, don't focus on the body. Instead, focus on the *nous*. Then you will know your true self. Then you will know God."

Joanna waited patiently for everyone to grasp this thought.

"Is this why Mary Magdalene spoke of the mind as the mischief-maker?" someone asked. "Because the mind neglects the *nous* and focuses instead on the body and worldly things?"

Joanna nodded. "Yes, exactly. This is why we must be vigilant every single day. The mind, the ego, focuses on your personal desires. For example, when you try to create happiness for yourself, that is a worldly desire. All worldly desires will not lead to happiness, but only to diversion and anxiety. True happiness comes from the soul, from the *nous*. Our bliss, our joy, is only found in the stillness of the *nous*. The mischief-maker leads us astray, away from the *nous*."

"Is the mischief-maker the same as the ego?" a girl asked.

Joanna nodded. "Yes, it is. Our ego is of this world, but it is not our true self. When I look at you, I do not see the real you, but an image of who I think you are. This image is your ego, but it is not your soul.

"The ego believes that it is real and that the world is real. This is where all of our desires come from, which ultimately create all of our problems. The solution to this predicament is to recognize and identify with the *nous*. This is why, as Perfecti, we detach from the world of matter and focus on the *nous*."

Joanna waited for a reply, but there was only silence, so she continued.

"Focusing on the *nous* allows God to show us the way. We become our own leaders. No longer do we trust the words of others, or even holy books such as the Bible. Now we lead ourselves, using God's inner direction. We no longer use rules, customs or scriptures—but instead, we follow the dictates of the *nous*. We follow God's direction."

"Perfecti Joanna, how do we know God's direction?" asked one of the girls.

Joanna smiled. "It's easy. Just listen to your heart—the *nous*—and not to anyone else. Whatever your heart tells you, that is the direction to go. I like to ask myself two questions to make sure guidance is truly coming from my heart: 1) Is this for the highest good? And 2) Is this in alignment with love?"

The girl who asked the question grimaced. "I often fear that I cannot trust myself, and that I will make the wrong decision."

"If you listen to your ego, then that is certainly possible. But if you listen to the *nous*, you will go in the right direction." Joanna smiled. "A Perfecti always knows the right direction."

"How do we know the difference?" one of the girls asked, still confused.

Joanna smiled and looked at her fellow Perfecti—Gilbert—who had been quietly standing by. "Perhaps you should answer this question, Gilbert. I seem to have confused them."

Gilbert nodded. "Sure. The first thing you need to understand is that there are two of you. There is the ego, which is the false self, and there is the real you, which is the soul. The ego is the chatter in your head. The ego wants you to think, because that is what keeps it alive. It wants you to think of the past and the future. It wants you to analyze your life and compare yourself to other people. What it really wants is for you to *identify* with this world. The ego wants you to be a worldly person with worldly thoughts.

"As Perfecti your only concern with the ego is keeping it at bay by being vigilant. This is done by paying attention to your thoughts and keeping them quiet. This is why you meditate every day. As Perfecti you want to focus on the *nous,* which is the real you. The *nous* is found in the stillness of the present moment. If you stay present, then you are always listening to your heart. It is easy to stay present when you understand that you are not your thoughts, but the awareness of your thoughts.

"In other words, when a thought pops into your mind, you have the capacity to stand back and look at that thought carefully. What is the motivation of the thought? Where did it come from? What is it's intention? What is it's potential outcome?

"As an aspiring Perfecti, you have to teach yourself to be vigilant, to be aware of your thoughts and if they are in alignment with love. Over time, you will teach yourself to only allow thoughts that are of service to your soul and of service to God. This is not easy to achieve, and why not everyone can become a Perfecti.

"All of you are becoming Perfecti. You are no longer focusing on the world. Now you are focusing on God. This makes love easy to obtain, because love is who we are—it is our core. It is the *nous.* The only thing that can take you away from the nous is the ego. Stay present, and the ego can be overcome. Stay present and you will find joy.

"When you learn to be aware with a still mind, then you will be gentle and in loving acceptance to those around you. This will allow you to spread love and live in joy. It is really quite simple, but the key is holding the ego—your false self—at bay. And the nous is the gateway to achieving that result. You have to learn to keep it open.

"What Joanna meant was that if you are focusing on the *nous* and not on the world, then it's easy to stay present and follow God's direction. Your devotion to God will make it easy to listen to your heart. All desire will be gone, except for the desire to help God and to live a pure life. However, you must be careful to not let the ego lead you astray.

"So," Gilbert continued, "if you want to know the difference, become aware of your desires. If you have any desires other than devotion to God, then your ego is interfering with your mission to become a Perfecti. It's really quite simple. If you focus on the *nous,* then God will guide you in that direction. If you focus on the ego, then God will guide you in that direction. It's your choice.

"As Perfecti, we are here to live a pure life. That can only be done by creating space between this world and the *nous*. When you are meditating that is what you are doing. You are creating space. You are going to the silence, to the *nous.* It is only when you identify with this world—the ego—that the *nous* is closed.

"You maintain your purity," Gilbert explained, "by always being aware of the space between this world—where our ego reigns—and the *nous*. As Perfecti, it is our destiny in life to maintain that space, to always be aware of it. This is our connection to spirit, to our soul, to the *nous*."

Gilbert stopped and there was silence as everyone pondered his eloquent answer.

"Did that answer your question?" Joanna asked, smiling, proud of Gilbert, and happy that he came today.

All of the girls nodded, as it was really quite clear now.

Joanna smiled at the group and rose.

"Okay, that is all for today," she said. "You still have some time to meditate before supper. Hopefully, this reinforced the importance of being devoted to God. Unless we spiritualize our life, we will not be ready for God's Kingdom."

CHAPTER TEN

Blanche and Robierre

Antoine, and several of Raymond's other knights, followed the Crusaders and watched Montfort subdue the remaining towns and villages in the Carcassonne region. By early spring of 1211, Montfort controlled the entire Carcassonne region, and had killed most of the Perfecti there.

Antoine rode into Château Narbonnais to give Raymond the bad news. He dismounted his horse, and walked with a determined step toward the castle doors to find Raymond.

He found him in his study, readying yet another scroll. He took two strides into the room and stood at attention.

"What is Montfort up to?" Raymond asked, putting down the scroll.

"My Lord, they have seized control of the entire Carcassonne region."

"I see. And what have you witnessed?" Raymond asked.

"Little, if any, resistance, my Lord. Each town has been accepting terms and giving Montfort the Perfecti. We witnessed burnings at St. Pons, Lazamet, Pezenas, and Lodève. He has not been leaving behind any of his mercenaries to secure the towns. Instead, he has threatened to come back and pillage any town that allows heresy to return. He told the town leaders to ensure that no heretics walk the streets. The local Catholic priest has become his spy."

Raymond rose from his chair and paced back and forth in contemplation, his long hair falling to his shoulders. As he analyzed the situation out loud, he looked down at the floor, as if deep in thought.

"It has taken him nearly two years to subdue Carcassonne, even though there has been very little resistance. Now he has fifty towns and villages that he must control. He doesn't have the manpower to control those towns. All he is using is threats."

"I agree, my Lord. There will be revolts."

Raymond nodded. "Until King Phillip Augustus decides on whom inherits Roger-Raymond Trencavel's land, the people will not accept Montfort and the Crusaders as the rulers. The people of Languedoc do not respect the Pope and his army, especially after what happened at Béziers."

"My Lord, do you expect the Crusaders to come to Lauragaise next?"

Raymond nodded. "Yes, we need to prepare."

"There is more, my Lord," Antoine said gravely.

Raymond stopped pacing and glared at Antoine, with an intensity that sent a chill up Antoine's spine. He waited impatiently for him to continue.

"You have been excommunicated, my Lord," Antoine sputtered nervously. "All of your lands have been confiscated. We heard it yesterday in Narbonne, on our way back to Toulouse."

Raymond was angry and resumed pacing. "I *thought* this might happen!" Raymond stated emphatically. "They confiscated Roger-Raymond Trencavel's land, and Montfort must have ambitions for taking all of my land, too."

After a moment of reflection, an old prediction came back to haunt him.

"Perfecti Pierre was right. For years he told me, over and over, that a war was coming to Languedoc to eliminate the Cathars. I always doubted him, because it seemed so preposterous – even though I knew him to be a very wise man.

"Antoine, come back tomorrow morning. We need to do some planning and preparations."

Antoine nodded, and responded quietly, "As you wish, my Lord," then turned and left.

* * * * *

A month later, Antoine watched with a few of his fellow knights, as Montfort marched toward Lavaur in Lauragaise. This was the event he had been waiting for. Now the crusade was moving to Lauragaise and the heart of the Cathars. Antoine and the knights all mounted their horses and rode quickly to Château Narbonnais.

Lavaur was only twenty miles from Toulouse, so it was not long before the knights rode through the gates of Raymond's castle. Antoine quickly dismounted and headed inside. As usual, he found Raymond in his study.

"What news do you bring, Antoine?" Raymond asked, sitting in his regal chair.

"My Lord, Montfort and the Crusaders are marching on Lavaur from the north. They have likely arrived by now. He also has a reinforcement army marching from the south towards Lavaur. I counted nearly a thousand men with Montfort. The reinforcements number a couple of hundred men."

Raymond realized that sitting and waiting was no longer the right strategy. It was time for him to make his first strike. He quickly arose and headed for the door.

"We will ride immediately and cut off those reinforcements!" he said. "We need to slow him down, before he reaches Toulouse."

Raymond VI and his army rode briskly to cut off the reinforcements in the south. And within a few hours, the first battle in Lauragaise took place. Raymond and his army prevailed, and cut down the reinforcement Crusaders.

The war in Languedoc between the nobles and Crusaders would last for nearly two more decades. Toulouse became the Cathars' most strategic and well-defended city. It was the most antagonistic towards the Crusaders. And it held the largest remaining population of Perfecti.

* * * * *

Blanche had her own small army of knights to defend her castle. When she heard of the siege of Lavaur, she sent a few of them to inquire. Lavaur was only twenty-five miles northwest of Laurac.

A few days later, her forces returned to the castle. Robierre, the head of her army, sought out Blanche to give her the bad news. He strode through the castle wearing his fortified armor. Over his long-sleeve tunic, he wore a light layer of steel netting that protected his chest and back during sword fighting. His clean black pants were made of leather that looked more for show than fighting, as did his spotless boots.

He found the Countess promptly, and stood at attention.

"What did you find, Robierre?" the Countess said anxiously, afraid of the answer.

"Countess, Lavaur has been conquered by the Crusaders. At least one hundred Perfecti were burned in a bonfire."[28]

Blanche sighed and stared at the floor in a state of shock. She closed her eyes and shuddered. Without looking up, she inquired further.

"Was the town spared, at least?" she asked, opening her eyes.

"Yes, only the defending knights and the Perfecti were killed. One hundred knights were put to the sword for resisting."

28 In April 1211, as many as 400 Cathar Perfecti were burned at the stake at Lavaur. This was perhaps the largest single annihilation of Cathars during the Albigensian Crusade.

"We need Raymond to help us!" she said angrily.

Robierre hesitated, letting Blanche calm down. "Countess, he has."

Blanche stared at him blankly. "What do you mean?"

"Raymond's army has attacked Montfort's reinforcements from the south, and has killed two hundred mercenaries. He has begun his defense."

Blanche smiled, optimism filling her heart. "At last! I knew that he would defend his lands. Ride to Château Narbonnais, and ask him if he needs my knights or any other help."

Robierre bowed and left the room.

* * * * *

A few weeks later, Antoine galloped towards Château Narbonnais to inform Raymond of Montfort's latest conquest.

Raymond was outside, decked out in battle gear, with his hundreds of horses and knights. They were already camped and preparing for battle. Everyone was ready for Raymond to give the word.

"My Lord," Antoine began, "Montfort has pillaged Montgey and burned it to the ground. Yesterday, he invaded Les Casses and burned twenty-five Perfecti."

Raymond motioned for Antoine to walk with him as he surveyed his knights and their preparations. "Montfort will be here soon. Stay here with me and help prepare the defenses."

It was apparent that Raymond was relaxed and confident. He held his helmet in

his right arm as they strode.

"The Counts of Foix and Comminges have arrived with their armies, and additional knights have been arriving courtesy of local nobles, as well. We have Montfort outnumbered and we are behind the walls. He cannot possibly win."

A few days later, on June 16th, 1211, the Crusaders laid siege to Toulouse. With only five hundred men, they were easily outmanned and out-positioned by Raymond's army. The Crusaders had little chance—and after a mere two weeks, they gave up the siege. No trebuchets were built and there were very few casualties on either side.

* * * * *

Robierre was behind the walls in Toulouse, helping in the defense as part of Raymond's army. After the siege, he returned to Laurac to inform Blanche about the outcome. Riding through the gates of Laurac Castle with his fellow knights, he felt confident for the first time in months. He dismounted assuredly, and walked toward the castle to find Blanche and give her the good news.

He found her outside in the garden, wearing a dark royal blue gown, watching her grandchildren playing in the afternoon sunshine. She seemed a perfect vision of a satisfied Countess, as she gazed upon the children, sunlight reflecting off of her jewelry.

He stood by and waited, while a servant took the children away.

"It wasn't much of a battle, Countess," Robierre said, once they were alone. "The Crusaders could not break through the walls, and only made a few attempts. After two weeks, they just gave up and marched south."

"Why did they give up so easily?" Blanche asked.

"Montfort must have known that we had a larger army. In fact, we could have attacked him and won. The Count of Foix was pressuring Raymond to attack after the first week."

"And why didn't he?" Blanche asked.

Robierre shrugged. "Raymond wanted to fight from behind the walls. Perhaps he was afraid to risk his position. A reinforcement army could have been waiting to counter-attack."

"What is to happen with Raymond's large army?" Blanche asked.

"They are planning to leave Toulouse and find Montfort. There is going to be another battle."

Blanche hesitated, unsure about exactly what this meant for their success. "Very well," she said. "Join them, and keep me informed."

Robierre nodded, and walked toward the castle.

"And don't get killed!" Blanche called after him, watching him go.

Robierre continued walking, but looked back at her, smiling. "I won't," he said cheerfully. "Who would protect you?"

* * * * *

About a month later, Robierre returned with more news for Blanche. Dejectedly, he dismounted his horse and walked to the castle. His face and clothes were dirty, and he was in dire need of a bath and something to eat.

He found Blanche and stood at attention. She came quickly, strode across the room to meet him.

"You look like you have been fighting. What happened?" she asked.

"Montfort invaded Castelnaudry a week ago. I was with Raymond's army when we heard the news. We quickly hurried to Castelnaudry and trapped Montfort behind the walls. The Crusaders numbered only five hundred to our thousand, and we thought we would defeat them with a calculated siege..."

Blanche could tell by the tone of his voice that something had gone wrong.

"Montfort won?" Blanche asked, distressed, cutting him off.

Robierre nodded. "Montfort is a skillful general, and he had reinforcements. We lost nearly a hundred knights, and Raymond withdrew."

"And where did Raymond take his army?" Blanche asked, still distressed.

"They are going to Tarn in Albige to recover the lands that the Crusaders recently conquered. His army is still larger than Montfort's. I'm sure there will be more battles. Tomorrow I will ride back and join them again."

Blanche nodded. "On your way to join Raymond, spread the news throughout the Lauragaise that Raymond's army endures. Let the nobles know that he is recapturing lands in Albige. If the people know that Raymond is resisting, they will support him."

Robierre bowed and left.

* * * * *

More than a year had passed, and Blanche decided to visit Montségur and inform Joanna and Gilbert of the current state of affairs. It was October 1212.

She rode alone to Montségur. It was not that far, only twenty miles to the south. The difficulty was the steep, nearly twenty minute hike to the top of the hill on which the fortress was located.

Blanche entered the gates and was greeted by several Perfecti in brown robes. They were surprised to see her traveling alone, and immediately directed her to Joanna's room. The fortress was busy, with over a hundred people loitering about in the courtyard. Perfecti had been arriving from all over Languedoc, seeking protection. She could smell bread being baked in the large oven that had been installed.

Blanche found Joanna's room and entered. There was no door, only a stone entrance.

"Mother!" Joanna exclaimed, rising to her feet and embracing Blanche. "I am so happy to see you. Do you bring good news?"

Joanna could see in her mother's face that she had not.

"Please sit, Mother," Joanna said, pointing to a wooden chair.

"It's not good," Blanche said, sitting down. "Montfort's army has been reinforced and is now bigger than Raymond's. Montfort has been going town to town, throughout the Lauragaise, and accepting terms of surrender. Hundreds of Perfecti have been burned. St. Michel de Lanes resisted, and Montfort burned it to the ground."

Joanna bowed her head dejectedly.

"Did they go back to Toulouse?" Joanna asked, looking up.

Blanche shook her head. "No. Raymond has set up his defense, and Montfort has been satisfied to conquer the rest of Lauragaise."

Joanna reflected on the situation for a moment, and then a sense of horror suddenly overcame her. "Oh, Mother! What of Laurac? What of my girls?" Joanna exclaimed in terror.

"Only three Perfecti have been burned in Laurac," Blanche answered, "and only men: Jean, Sebastion, and René. The Crusaders did not find the Women's Home. The girls are now safe, as the Crusaders have left."

"That is dreadful, but thank goodness my girls are okay," Joanna said, in relief. "Where is Montfort now?"

"He is north in the Agenais Region. After he left Lauragaise, he pillaged the towns along the Tarn. St. Marcel pleaded for terms, but Montfort was still angry from a futile siege a few months earlier, and so he burned it to the ground. The same fate awaited Laguépie. At St. Antonin, the people attempted to flee. But Montfort tracked them all down like animals, as they ran, and murdered everyone he could find."

"Mother, he is a barbarian! I can't believe that this is supposed to be a *Christian* crusade." Joanna began sobbing, and quickly became nearly hysterical. "Why is so much murder happening?"

At that moment, Gilbert came into the room. He placed his hand gently on Joanna's shoulder to comfort her. "These are the ways of Satan," he said calmly. "It is not for us to combat evil with evil. Tears, anger and resentment do no good, Joanna. Only love can spread light and smother the dark."

His words began to calm and comfort her. "Remember Joanna, the mind is the mischief-maker. When you harbor anger, you are creating darkness. Your anger only creates more war. Our thoughts and actions need to be in alignment with love."

Joanna took a deep breath, and felt a deep sense of relief as she gazed into Gilbert's eyes. Then she knelt down, and prayed silently for a couple of minutes. When she arose, she spoke calmly. "Thank you, Gilbert. I will meditate on this tonight. And I will send light to Montfort and the Crusaders."

Gilbert grinned. "Very good."

Gilbert turned to Blanche. "Hello Countess. Walking down the hall, I overheard you say that Montfort and the Crusaders are pillaging Languedoc, and continuing to kill the Perfecti."

Blanche nodded. "There is more," she said sadly. "Do you wish to hear it?"

Gilbert nodded, and sat down in the other wooden chair. "Yes, we need to stay informed. There will be many Perfecti coming here for asylum."

"After Tarn, Montfort turned north to the Agenais region. Agenais is virtually free of Cathars, yet it is wealthy and part of Raymond VI's land. Montfort found a defended fortress at Penne d'Agenais and laid siege. It began in June and lasted six weeks. Unfortunately, the fortress walls were no match for Montfort's large trebuchets.

"After Penne d'Agenais, Montfort attacked Moissac and Montauban. Both are strategically placed towns at river crossings. Moissac has high walls, and was vigorously defended, but Montfort's army was too strong. During the siege, the surrounding towns and villages sent terms to Montfort, surrendering before he even arrived. Once the siege ended at Moissac, the defending knights and mercenaries were put to the sword. The people paid

Montfort in gold not to destroy the town. He accepted ownership of the town and did not destroy it."

Blanche shook her head in disgust. "Not even one Perfecti was found! This was supposed to be a crusade, but it's turning into a war over land!

"Anyway, the siege at Moissac lasted until late September. With winter approaching, Montfort did not lay siege to Montauban. Instead, he marched to his castle in Pamiers and called for a council.

"He now controls nearly all of Languedoc. All of the major towns, except Toulouse and Montauban, have accepted terms. I'm sure the council will attempt to consolidate his power."

As Blanche stopped, the situation seemed bleak, indeed. "Do you have any questions?"

"Do you think that Raymond can hold Toulouse?" Gilbert asked.

Blanche close her eyes and contemplated. When she opened them, tears had welled up. "I don't know. I fear that is the next battle. If Toulouse falls, we lose our way of life. All is lost."

Gilbert knew that she was right. If Toulouse fell, surely Montségur would be next.

CHAPTER ELEVEN

Antoine and Raymond

Antoine had been sent to Pamiers by Raymond to find out the outcome of the council. After the council adjourned, he returned to Château Narbonnais to inform Raymond.

Riding across the moat and through the gates, he knew that Raymond would not be pleased. He dismounted his horse and handed the reigns to a servant. His knightly uniform glistened in the morning sun. He wore no armor that day, but his sparkly silver tunic still shone from a distance.

As usual, he found Raymond in his study, reading in his favorite chair. "What news do you bring, Antoine?" Raymond asked, placing a scroll on his lap.

"My Lord, the council has adjourned. As you predicted, the Catholic bishops changed the laws of Languedoc. They are calling it the Statute of Pamiers.[29] It was signed on December 1st."

"And what does it contain?" Raymond asked.

"Taxation has been halted, thereby preventing you from collecting any money from your vassals..."

"Those bastards!" Raymond exclaimed angrily. "They did that so people can tithe to the Catholic Church. Instead of taxes going to the nobles, now they go to the Church."

"What else?" Raymond asked dejectedly.

---

29 Simon de Monfort convened a council at Pamiers in December 1212 to implement and replace an assortment of laws.

"Well, the secular powers in each town and village are commanded to deliver all heretics to the Church for punishment and to confiscate their property. Also, the Church has dictated that attendance of Catholic mass on Sunday is now compulsory."

Raymond grunted. "They're going to try to *force* their religion on us, is that it? I don't think that is going to work. Anything else in the statute, Antoine?"

"No, my Lord."

"Well, at least they didn't give my lands to anyone. Even if they did, only King Phillip Augustus has the right to do that. The King has already written the Pope, and told him that he can have his crusade, but the Monarchy is not giving up its sovereignty. I am the King's vassal, and Raymond VII is now old enough to inherit my lands. Now that Raymond VII has married the sister of Peter II of Aragon, the King will not want to lose this strong family under his empire."

"Unless the King desires your land, my Lord."

Raymond was taken aback for a moment, and glanced at Antoine. "Yes, I fear you might be right about that, Antoine. This crusade could provide the King with the opportunity to lay claim to all of Languedoc."

"We'll just have to defeat the crusade to prevent that from happening."

Raymond nodded.

* * * * *

A couple of months later, in early 1213, a Perfecti visited Montségur with incredible news.

"Gilbert, the crusade is over!" the visitor exclaimed. "The Pope has given the Counts back their lands, and has stopped the crusade. We can finally return home and do our spiritual work again!"

Gilbert smiled at the glad tidings, but had reservations. "No, not yet," he said. "I don't trust this Pope. Let us wait a few months for confirmation. But thank you for the news. Let us pray that this truly is the final outcome."

A few days later, Gilbert and Joanna went to visit Blanche in Laurac, to discuss the recent development.

Blanche met them at the castle gate, welcoming Joanna with open arms and a warm smile. "You broke your promise again. I didn't say that it was safe to leave Montségur."

"We have been told that the crusade is over!" Joanna said, embracing her mother.

Blanche shook her head in disappointment, and began walking toward the castle. Gilbert and Joanna walked alongside the Countess. It was a cold winter day and they all wore heavy cloaks.

"Yes, it was stopped, but for only a short time," Blanche said. "The Pope heard about the Statute of Pamiers, and thought that Montfort had conquered all of Languedoc. He thought that the crusade was no longer necessary. Then Montfort convinced him that he was not finished, and it has resumed."

"We heard that the Pope had returned all of the confiscated land back to the Counts," Gilbert said doubtfully.

"He did! And now he has taken it all back!" Blanche shook her head slowly. "I don't know why. Raymond thinks that the Pope thought he had enough control of Languedoc, along with the Statute of Pamiers, to eradicate the heretics. Then he realized that he had made a big mistake, and he went right back to the crusade."

"I'm tired of all this talk of war," Joanna said. "I came to see you, Mother, and to visit my girls at the Perfecti Women's Home."

Blanche smiled. "Come inside to get warm and have something to eat first. Then you can go visit your girls. Tomorrow, I want you to return to Montségur."

"Yes, Mother," Joanna said, in perfect obedience.

* * * * *

After a quick lunch, Gilbert and Joanna walked to the Women's Home. When they arrived on that cold winter's day, it was a big surprise to the girls.

"Perfecti Joanna's here!" exclaimed one of the girls.

"Oh good, I have questions!" said another girl excitedly.

"Are you going to teach a lesson?" asked another.

By now, all of the girls were in the front room, greeting Joanna.

Joanna smiled. "Of course. Don't I always? I'm sorry that I've been away for so long."

Joanna and Gilbert removed their cloaks. The room was warm from a large fire in the fireplace. Each of the girls had already found a comfortable place to sit. The excitement in the room was unmistakable. The girls were delighted to once again be learning something new from Joanna.

Joanna sat down. "I guess we will have the lesson here today, since it is so comfortable with the fire. Is it freezing in the teaching room?"

The girls laughed. "Yes," they replied, not wanting to leave.

"Who had a question?" Joanna asked.

One of the girls raised her hand. "I've been thinking about what you talked about last time. About the *nous,* and how our connection to our soul links us to God's soul—how everything is interrelated. In Ephesians 4:13 it states: '*It is inherent in our faith that in the end we will all attain Oneness through Gnosis of God's Son, becoming fully initiated human beings, equal to nothing less than the pleroma of Christ.*' I think I understand, but can you explain this passage?"

Joanna grinned, excited to be asked about her favorite scripture. "Certainly. This is one of the few passages in the New Testament that speaks of Gnosis. Most of the Gnostic references have been expunged from the Bible, and can only be found in the Gnostic Gospels. This passage refers to the meaning of life and reincarnation.

"When it states 'in the end,' that is a reference to the end of the reincarnation cycle. At that point, we will have achieved oneness with the soul of God. We will look upon mankind and see only our reflections. Our awareness will be so profound as to equal that of Christ. We will be enlightened."

"Is that what it means to be fully initiated?" the same girl asked.

"Yes. Initiation is simply a learning process. For instance, when we learn something new, that is an initiation. Each time we accomplish something, that is an initiation. To be fully initiated is to be fully awakened to the *nous*.

"Even Christ, in his final incarnation, was initiated. He spent most of his life preparing for his ministry. In fact, it was not until the very end of his life that he preached to the masses. Mary Magdalene speaks of Jesus' initiations in Egypt in her Gospel. He continued to become fully initiated until his final days."

"That means," the girl replied, "that, even though we are God, we are always learning, always being initiated. It is a never ending journey of enlightenment."

Joanna nodded. "Yes, we are all God finding our way back home. As you all know, that is not easy. In fact, enlightenment occurs rarely.

"I may be called a Perfecti, but that does necessarily mean that I am enlightened, or that I will not incarnate again. To be fully initiated is a long process that requires much diligence and care. And, it is only achieved through unyielding deliberate intent and devotion to God."

"At some point, the journey turns inward?" asked another girl.

Joanna nodded. "Yes. Of course it does. The outer world is not where we find God, although that is where our journey begins. This is the first place the ego – the mind – looks for God. At some point, however, you have to give up searching in vain, because the world of matter is an illusion. If you try to find God in the world, you will be searching in the wrong place. That is why we meditate.

"We go within to find the *nous*. Joanna placed her hand over her heart area. This is our link to God's soul. This is where we find God and the source of love. As Mary Magdalene's gospel states, 'I go now into silence.' It is the silence of our consciousness that is the doorway to God. It is the doorway to our true self."

Another girl raised her hand. "In the Gnostic Gospel, The Treatise on the Resurrection, it states: '*The cosmos is an illusion. The resurrection is the revelation of what is.*'[30] Since Jesus resurrected as spirit, isn't this passage a reference to what you are saying?"

Joanna nodded. "Yes. The cosmos – the world – is an illusion. The spirit world is what is real. Our connection to spirit is where our true identity resides. This is the link of the *nous*, to our inner consciousness."

Gilbert raised his hand to offer another reference for the girls. "There is an excellent reference in the Gospel of Phillip," he commented. "It states: '*Even if the physical world moves, I shall not move. Even if it is destroyed, I shall not be destroyed. For the light is me and I am the light.*'"[31]

The room was silent for several seconds.

"That is beautiful," Joanna said. "Does everyone understand it fully? It says that if the world is destroyed, it doesn't effect us. Why? Because we are not of the world, we are of the light. The light is in me! The light is in you! The light is the *nous*. This is our

30 *The Treatise on the Resurrection*, NHC, 1.4.45-6.

31 *Pistis Sophia*, 2.33.

connection to God, our connection to each other. This, literally, is how we find our way to the Kingdom of God."

"Is the light our soul?" a girl asked.

Joanna nodded. "Yes, it is the energy of our soul. It can illuminate to such magnificence that the human eye cannot bear it. We are all beacons of light. It is what gives us consciousness. It is what gives us life. Our soul is literally a spark of God."

"Perfecti Joanna, I am afraid," one of the girls confessed, in a tormented voice. "I hear your beautiful words, but I don't see how I can become a Perfecti in this lifetime. I fear that I will reincarnate again into Satan's world. How do I know that Satan will not tempt me in my next life?"

"There is nothing to worry about," Joanna said soothingly. "There is a scripture that speaks of this. It is in The Book of the Savior.

"It states: '*In its next birth, the good psyche will not be given the draught of oblivion, but will be cast back into a body which will not be able to fall asleep and forget. It will be ever pure of heart, seeking after the Mysteries of Light until it has found them.*'[32]

"So, you see.... If you begin your journey to find God, to find the light, you will continue that journey in your next life. It is guaranteed. You will not regress."

The girl smiled joyously. "Thank you, Perfecti, Joanna."

"Anyone else?" Joanna asked.

"When will we know that we are enlightened?" another girl asked.

Joanna hesitated and then recited slowly, from memory, what she was taught by Pierre. "When our consciousness is aware that the world is an illusion and we no longer identify with it. Instead, we identify with our greater truth, which is that

32 *Jesus and the Lost Goddess*, Timothy Freke and Peter Gandy, Three Rivers Press, 2001, p. 111.

our true self is made of spirit. At that point, we will we become one with God."

She paused for a moment to allow the students to process this difficult and abstract concept.

"Once this happens, we become gentle, nurturing, accepting, and non-reactive to the world around us. We become walking angels, and pure of heart."

There was more silence as the girls still struggled to understand. Finally, one was able to form a specific question.

"What do you mean by one with God?" she asked.

"Let's do a quick experiment," Joanna said. "Everyone close your eyes. Take a deep breath and focus your attention on your hands. Feel the tingling sensation. That is the energy of the soul! That is your life force! Notice how your mind is silent as you feel your hands—that is how you open the channel to the *nous* and become one with God.

"Now, transfer the energy in your hands up your arms so that you feel the energy move. Continue moving the energy up your arms, up your neck, and out of your head, shooting all the way up to God's Kingdom. Imagine that the source of your consciousness is tethered in God's Kingdom. Imagine that your soul is literally in heaven, yet connected to you through the *nous* of consciousness. When you open your eyes, imagine that your soul in heaven can now see, hear, and touch the world through your body.

"Okay, open your eyes. What you are now seeing is being watched and heard from heaven by your higher self. Thus, the source of your consciousness does not reside in your body. It resides in heaven. This is the same for everyone, and it is the same source that we all share!

"The *nous* is not only the gateway of the soul, but it is also the source of love. You can use it to be consumed by love. You can literally pull love through the *nous* and into your body. Imagine a stream of love traveling through the *nous* into your body. By doing this you can purify yourself and raise your vibration. A wise Perfecti does this every day.

"Okay girls," Joanna said, getting up, "that is enough for today. I'll leave you with that thought, and we can discuss it again next time. Now, everyone go and meditate and find the *nous*. Once you find it, you will have found the source of who you really are, and your connection to God."

* * * * *

Robierre rode into the castle and hurried to see Blanche. It was September 1213. The third battle between Raymond's army and the Crusaders had just ended.

Robierre was dejected. He had hoped that they could defeat Montfort, but they had lost for the second time. Now he walked with trepidation, fearing that there were even more battles to be lost.

He found the Countess and stood at attention. His soiled clothes revealed the long battle which he had just endured.

"Robierre, what news do you bring?" Blanche asked anxiously, seeing his somber expression.

"Countess, Montfort has won another battle at Muret. Peter II of Aragon was killed, and Raymond's army was badly weakened. I'm sorry, but the resistance army has dispersed. The Counts of Comminges and Foix have returned home with their armies. Raymond is at Toulouse with his knights and mercenaries."

"What about Montfort and the Crusaders?" Blanche asked fearfully. The bad news was making her feel physically ill.

"I think they are strong enough to attack Toulouse now. If he captures Toulouse, he will have complete control of Languedoc."

Blanche shuddered.

* * * * *

For the next few months, Raymond prepared to defend Toulouse with his badly weakened army. Finally, in April 1214, Raymond found out why the attack had not been launched. The Pope had halted the crusade for the second time.

Antoine had heard the news in Toulouse and hurried to Château Narbonnais to inform Raymond. He found Raymond in his study.

"What is it, Antoine?" Raymond asked, not looking up from his scroll.

"My Lord, the Pope has sent a legate to Carcassonne.[33] His name is Peter of Benevento, and he has halted the crusade. All of the nobles have been summoned to meet with him. The rumor is that he is going to ask you to surrender and accept his terms."

Raymond dropped the scroll, and got up from his chair with a look of concern. "Never! But without Peter's army [Peter II of Aragon], and if the Counts of Comminges and Foix accept terms, I cannot defend Toulouse."

Antoine hesitated, and then made a bold suggestion. "Go into exile, my Lord. There is always another day for a battle."

Raymond nodded. "That is good advice. I will go to Spain and collect mercenaries, and prepare for another battle. Let the Pope think that he has won, and he will stop paying his mercenaries. He must be getting tired of paying for this crusade. I'm sure he would love to disband his army and start collecting tithes, instead.

"Let him think he has won," Raymond mused again. "There are a hundred nobles I can count on to support me when I return. This war is still not over."

33 In the spring of 1214, Pope Innocent III sent Cardinal Peter of Benevento to Carcassonne to negotiate a settlement of Languedoc.

CHAPTER TWELVE

The Siege of Toulouse

In December 1215, Blanche went to visit Montségur. It had been months since she had seen Joanna.

It was a cold day, and the hike up the steep hill was difficult as usual. Walking through the gates, she was surprised to see even more Perfecti than on her last visit. Montségur was teeming with people. The first few Perfecti she saw did not recognize her, but then several of the Perfecti began to bow to her and call her Countess.

Blanche continued on through the bustling courtyard and into the monastery's entrance. Inside, she found Gilbert in the hallway.

"Countess, it is good to see you. Are you looking for Joanna?"

Blanche nodded. "Yes, do you know where she is?"

"This way," Gilbert said, leading her down the stone hallway. "There is no heat in most of the rooms. So, in the winter, the Perfecti stay in the great room where it is warm. We only return to our rooms to sleep."

Blanche remembered that the great room was very large, and when they entered they found more than fifty people; yet, it was nowhere close to being full.

The room was a lengthy rectangle with a high lofted ceiling. Two long rows of tables and benches were aligned from one end of the room to the other, and many people were seated at the tables and were eating.

At each end of the room, there were large fireplaces that kept the entire room warm. A dozen chairs were situated near both of the fires, and many of those seats were occupied, too.

Gilbert and Blanche entered near the center of the room, and walked toward one of the fires. Joanna saw them approaching, and she quickly rose to run and hug her mother.

"Mother it has been ages!" Joanna said, after they had exchanged a lengthy and emotional embrace.

Gilbert pointed to an unoccupied table. "Let's go sit over there."

"What can you tell us of the crusade?" Joanna asked, with trepidation, as they walked to the table.

Blanche removed her cloak and sat comfortably. As usual, she was the best-dressed person in the room. Even in the dead of winter and after a strenuous hike up a formidable hill, she looked regal. She definitely looked like a Countess.

Blanche straightened the neat bun on the back of her head. The lovely, silken gold ribbon around the bun was perfectly tied.

"The crusade was halted several months ago," Blanche stated. "Raymond went into exile in Spain, and the rest of the nobles surrendered. However, Montfort's army was not disbanded. He has continued to march his small army around Languedoc, mostly just to intimidate everyone.

Her demeaning tone indicated that she thought very little of the man.

"I'm sorry that I did not visit this summer," she said, "but it has been much too dangerous to travel."

"Have they been burning Perfecti?" Gilbert asked.

"Very few, thank God. He has had his hands full just keeping the nobles in order. They keep moving back into their castles and rebuilding their armies! All of Languedoc is becoming rebellious.

The people do not support Montfort. And King Phillip has never validated his claims on Languedoc. We are still the vassals of the King, not the Pope, and everyone knows it."

"What about Toulouse?" Gilbert asked.

"He has avoided it, so far," Blanche replied. "Montfort's army is small—less than five hundred men—and Toulouse would resist, even without Raymond."

Gilbert nodded. "Where is Raymond—in Spain, you said?"

"Yes. He is in Spain, gathering mercenaries. However, his son—Raymond VII—is preparing to defend Toulouse. He is old enough now to fight, and he has taken charge of the army that Raymond VI left behind."

Gilbert nodded. "Is the crusade going to resume?"

"Yes, it's very likely. The Pope will *have* to attack Toulouse, sooner or later, in order to achieve his goals. There are still hundreds of Perfecti left in Toulouse, and he knows it. I think it's inevitable that Raymond VI and VII are going to do battle with Montfort soon. Both of you should stay here, where you are safe."

Joanna shuddered, and said what all three were thinking. "The Pope is slowly and methodically squeezing all of Languedoc. I don't think he will stop until he has killed every Perfecti."

* * * * *

The next month, more bad news came to Château Narbonnais. A courier from Carcassonne arrived at the gate, and Antoine was summoned. After hearing the dire news, he solemnly sought out Raymond VII in the castle.

He found the young, nineteen-year-old Raymond VII wearing his knightly battle regalia, inside the great room, the largest room in the castle. He was with his young wife and several servants.

Antoine approached Raymond VII.

"What is it, Antoine?" Raymond VII inquired.

"My Lord, we have news from Italy," Antoine said gravely.

The young Lord scanned the room as he sternly commanded those present, "Please leave us now. I must attend to my affairs."

His wife hurried out of the room, holding her gown to prevent it from dragging on the floor. And the servants left right behind her.

"Please continue," Raymond VII said, with a sense of urgency.

"The Pope has held a council at Lateran in Italy,"[34] Antoine said. "Your father was there, and pleaded for your inheritance rights. But his efforts failed. It was decided that you cannot inherit your father's land."

"Then *who* will get the land?" Raymond VII asked apprehensively.

"It was not decided. Perhaps Montfort. Perhaps the Pope. Maybe even the King."

"Then we will fight!" Raymond VII said angrily. "Prepare the army to march. We are going to take the castle of Beaucaire away from the Crusaders. Then we will defend it against Montfort!"

Antoine was surprised. "Why Beaucaire? It is over a hundred miles to the east."

Young Raymond's passion was evident. There was no fear in his voice. "That is where my grandfather was born. That is my family's true home. I will go there and take what is mine!"

"Very well, my Lord." Antoine nodded and left the room.

* * * * *

Several months passed, and it was now late August of 1216. Robierre witnessed the outcome at Beaucaire, and rode to inform Blanche. It was a hundred-mile ride. Beaucaire was located far east of Laurac on the Rhône River, just south of Avignon.

He arrived back in Laurac, and rode through the castle gates, confident once again. Every time they lost a battle to the

34 The Fourth Lateran Council met in November 1215 and ruled against Raymond VII.

Crusaders, he thought that there was no hope left. But then time would pass, and the war would continue on without a Crusader triumph. Now he felt hope, once more, that victory might eventually come to their side.

Robierre dismounted from his horse and walked purposefully to the castle. His clothes were clean this time. He had not fought in the battle, but had merely watched it from a distance.

He found the Countess alone in her sitting room and stood at attention. This was a rather small room, where the Countess liked to come for tea in the afternoon.

"Do you bring news from Beaucaire?" Blanche asked, sipping her tea. She was looking as beautiful as ever, with nary a hair out of place, the bun on the back of her head perfectly coifed.

Robierre nodded. "Countess, Montfort has surrendered and accepted terms from Raymond VII at Beaucaire."

Blanche was quite amazed, and raised her eyebrows. "Tell me about the battle?"

"Beaucaire is located on a steep cliff above the Rhône. It is also protected by high walls on its other three sides. Raymond VII laid siege to the town in April. The Crusaders and the townspeople inside were able to hold him off.

"Then in June, Montfort arrived with reinforcements and laid siege to young Raymond's besiegers. I thought that young Raymond was pinched and that he would surely lose, but he held his position with resolve. It was Montfort who surrendered the town and accepted terms."

Blanche chuckled to herself, putting down her porcelain cup. "It looks like he's a better general than his father," she said jokingly.

Robierre did not smile in return, but looked somewhat anxious.

"What is it, Robierre?" Blanche asked, concerned.

"Well, the Crusaders were not weakened, and they marched away safely. I don't think the terms actually favored Raymond VII to any extent."

Blanche pondered this. "You are probably right, Robierre. This means that Montfort will simply strengthen his army and attack again. We can only hope that Raymond VI returns from Spain with more mercenaries."

"One last thing, Countess. Pope Innocent III has died in Rome."[35]

Blanche was surprised again, and hesitated before offering any comment. She reached down and took a sip of tea. "Well, well..." she said thoughtfully. "This could be a momentous day. Our two biggest enemies have suffered defeats. Maybe things are starting to go our way. Perhaps the next Pope will not be interested in pursuing this unreasonable crusade."

Robierre grinned. "Time will tell."

* * * * *

Raymond VII remained at Beaucaire after his victory. Montfort, being the intelligent general that he was, immediately marched one hundred and twenty miles to Toulouse, in the west, and attacked. He knew it was defenseless.

A courier rode into Beaucaire and informed Antoine of the situation in Toulouse. He immediately sought out young Raymond VII.

"My Lord, Montfort has attacked Toulouse. He has arrested most of the town's noblemen, and placed a tax on every house and business. The buildings without payments are being marked with an X and then destroyed. He is extorting the city for a treasure of silver."

"And he is destroying it!" Raymond VII said angrily.

"Should we prepare the army to march, my Lord?"

35 Pope Innocent III died on July 16th, 1216.

Raymond VII hesitated. "No. We're staying here until my father returns. We will wait for Father, and then attack the Crusaders."

Antoine bowed and turned to leave.

"Did Montfort burn any Perfecti in Toulouse?" Raymond VII asked.

Antoine turned back and shook his head. "No, my Lord. He was only after silver."

"Interesting," Raymond VII said. "After all these years of crusading, he finally gets his chance at Toulouse, and he doesn't kill any Perfecti."

Antoine smiled at the thought, and then shrugged his shoulders. "Since the crusade is currently halted, perhaps he is only fighting for the control of Languedoc. If Montfort gains control, he can always let the Catholics burn the remaining Perfecti."

Raymond VII nodded. "Clearly, he wanted the silver to pay for his mercenaries. He knows that this war is not over."

* * * * *

Nearly a year went by before Raymond VI returned. In September of 1217, Raymond VI rode into Château Narbonnais with an entourage of five hundred Spanish mercenary knights. Montfort had moved on months ago, and had not left any mercenaries in Toulouse to defend the town.

Raymond VII heard of his father's imminent return, and he had marched to Château Narbonnais ahead of his father.

Raymond VI dismounted his horse and smiled at his waiting son. Father and son embraced after their lengthy separation. Then Raymond VI faced his twenty-year-old son and gripped his shoulders. The Count's clean blue cassock with gold embroidery, thick wool pants, and tall boots revealed his true stature.

"You have done well, my son," Raymond VI said, smiling.

Raymond VII demurred. "But I did not defend Toulouse, Father. And much has been destroyed."

"You faced Montfort and defeated him!" Raymond VI exclaimed. "You have done nothing wrong. We will fight together now and destroy his army."

Raymond VI was obviously feeling jubilant and optimistic. He put his arm around his son's neck and they walked toward the castle together.

"Are you ready for a big battle?" Raymond VI asked, his long hair falling to his shoulders.

Raymond VII smiled. "I am ready to win, Father."

"Good," Raymond VI said, smiling. "The Counts of Foix and Comminges are sending their armies. We will be well prepared. This is going to be the biggest battle of the crusade!"

* * * * *

Montfort laid siege to Toulouse in October. Robierre was getting on in years, but he watched the battle from a safe vantage point. Every week, he rode to nearby Laurac to inform Blanche about Montfort's progress.

Each time he rode through the castle gates, Blanche was informed of his arrival. She always waited for him in the great room. Each time he arrived, Blanche found that she was far too nervous to speak, so she usually just nodded.

"The battle continues, Countess. Raymond's crossbows have been effective, so far, in preventing the Crusaders from entering Toulouse and breaching the walls. Both sides now have trebuchets, and are hurling each other's stones back and forth. They battle on daily. Each side is sustaining losses. But this could go on for months."

"Who has the advantage?" Blanche asked apprehensively.

"I would say Raymond, since he is behind the walls, but Montfort has a large and determined army. It is hard to say."

"What would you estimate is the size of each army?" Blanche asked.

"Perhaps one thousand knights on each side. It's fairly even in numbers."

Blanche nodded. "Keep me informed.

* * * * *

On June 25th, 1218, Robierre rode through the Laurac Castle gates jubilantly. After months of continuous fighting to a stalemate, it was over. He marched confidently to the great room to inform Blanche of the wonderful news.

Robierre could hardly contain his happiness. "Montfort is dead!" he declared loudly to Blanche, before she had even acknowledged his presence.

"What happened, Robierre?" Blanche asked.

"It's over! Finally, after *nine* months of warfare! And Raymond has won! Montfort was killed by a trebuchet stone.[36] The Crusaders are marching south, defeated!"

"Ring the bells," Blanche said to a servant with a subdued tone. It was time to celebrate the moment. But she was not confident that it was over. The new Pope could always send another army.

"Were there any terms?" Blanche asked, still concerned.

"I don't think so—but they no longer have a general!"

"Ah, but he will be replaced. It's not over, Robierre," Blanche said seriously.

Robierre suddenly felt like an old fool. She was right, of course. It was too soon to celebrate. There were no terms.

Blanche saw the disappointment on Robierre's face. "Well, hopefully the new Pope will not reinforce the Crusaders. If they

36 It's interesting that Monfort died nine years after the Crusade began, and after a nine month siege. In numerology, nine is the number of endings.

stay at their present strength, Raymond has proven that he can withstand their force."

Robierre grinned. "Yes, Countess. Raymond's army is formidable."

Blanche knew that she was just hoping. Pierre's prediction that all of the Perfecti would be killed still haunted her.

"That is all, Robierre."

He bowed and left the room.

CHAPTER THIRTEEN

The Crusade is Paused—1219

In early 1219, Blanche went to visit Montségur. Walking up the steep hill, she wondered how many more years she could do this. The hike was challenging for her. She had to stop frequently to take rest breaks, but finally she reached the top.

She entered the tall fortress gates, and found her way to the great hall. It was a very cold day, so she had decided to look for Joanna in the warmth of the fireplaces. She quickly spotted her daughter, talking to some friends, and met her with a warm smile of optimism.

"Mother!" Joanna exclaimed, rising to greet her with a hug. "It is so good to see you!"

Joanna had been sitting with a group of fellow Perfecti near one of the fires. She led Blanche to an unoccupied table, so that they could be alone.

Blanche removed her heavy cloak and sat down, this time revealing a sumptuous red dress that made her look exceedingly attractive. Many people might have thought it inappropriate for her to wear red, when so many dear friends around her had been dying. But Blanche enjoyed wearing brightly colored clothes and looking the part of a Countess.

Joanna sat down across from her. "Mother, we have been hearing good news," Joanna said excitingly. "Is it true that Perfecti are preaching once again in Languedoc?"

Blanche was subdued, and did not return Joanna's excitement. "Yes, that is true," she said. "For the first time since the crusade began in 1209, Perfecti are preaching in public. I have heard accounts in Carcassonne, Narbonne, all of the Lauragaise, Albige. Everywhere."

"Mother, that is great news," Joanna said with enthusiasm. Then she saw the look of worry on her mother's face. "It *is* great, isn't it? What is it, Mother?"

"The new Pope, Honorius III, has manipulated King Phillip into leading the crusade. As you know, this is what Pierre always dreaded. He said that if the Pope and the King ever united, then the nobles could not resist their combined power. It would be the end of the Cathars."

Joanna reflected quietly on her mother's words.

At that moment, Gilbert walked over. "Hello, Countess," he said with a bow. "Why the dour faces? What has happened?" he asked, sitting down next to Joanna.

Joanna looked at him solemnly. "Mother has just told me that King Phillip is going to lead the crusade."

Gilbert was shocked by the bad news. "What else can you tell us, Countess?"

"Pope Honorius has been negotiating with King Phillip Augustus ever since Montfort was killed and the crusade was halted last summer. King Phillip rejected him at first. But then Honorius offered Thibault IV – the Count of Champagne – the chance to lead the crusade. Thibault accepted, thinking that he could take control of the Languedoc and add it to his fiefdom.[37]

"In light of these events, the King had no choice but to push Thibault aside and take charge of the crusade himself. The Pope has told the King that all he wants is an end to the Cathars. The

37 King Phillip Augustus and Thibault IV had no quarrel with the Cathars, they just wanted more power.

Pope does not care if the King lays claim to all of the lands in Languedoc."

Gilbert sighed. "That is not good. Languedoc has not had a legal owner since the crusade began. It is there for the taking. Now the King has a chance to claim all of southern France and add it to his empire. All he has to do is help the Catholic Church eliminate us. The people will gladly accept his rule, instead of the Pope's henchmen."

There was a long period of silence, and Joanna was suddenly struck by the severity of the situation. "Oh, my God. We are doomed," she said pessimistically.

"Let us not give up yet," Blanche said. "Raymond still has a large army."

Gilbert nodded. "As long as Raymond has an army, we still have a chance."

"Joanna, stay here," Blanche said. "King Phillip's son, Louis VIII, is going to lead the crusade. His army will be arriving soon, and I would feel better if you were here."

"Yes, Mother."

* * * * *

In late spring, 1219, Robierre watched as Louis VIII marched toward Languedoc. He was terrified. The Royal Army marched with more than five hundred men on horses, plus another two thousand men on foot! Wearing their battle regalia and carrying their arsenal of weapons, they presented an imposing image.

Robierre waited for the outcome of Louis VIII's first conquest, and then headed for Laurac. Riding through the gates, he was even more dejected than on his past trips home. How could he tell her? This was what the Countess had always feared.

He found her sitting in the great room in a beautiful, gold-colored gown, touched with tinges of orange and copper. He stood near the entrance of the room in his knight's uniform, waiting for her to address him.

"Has Louis VIII's army arrived in Languedoc?" she asked.

He nodded. "His army is huge, Countess. He completely surrounded Marmande and then attacked. From what I saw, everyone was killed, and then the entire town was burned to the ground."[38]

"Everyone?" Blanche asked, terrified. "The women and children?"

Robierre nodded. "When Louis arrived, Arnaud Amaury[39] had been laying siege with his small Crusading army of two hundred men. I guess Louis wanted to set an example of what happens to resisters."

Blanche shuddered. "Could this happen at Toulouse?"

"We are going to find out. That is where he is marching now."

Blanche looked horrified. "Oh, my God!"

* * * * *

Antoine watched from behind the walls of Toulouse as Louis VIII and Arnaud Amaury marched the Crusaders into position. They laid siege by completely encircling the town. He climbed down from one of Toulouse's stalwart walls and made his way to Raymond VI and Raymond VII.

He found them together, both wearing their knightly battle regalia, ready to fight.

"My Lords, the Crusaders have us surrounded. It is quite a large army," said Antoine.

"Prepare the defenses. There will be no terms," Raymond VI said firmly.

---

38 The Albigensian Crusade is well documented by historians. Every battle in this book and the described outcomes actually occurred.

39 Arnaud Amaury had resumed leading the crusade after Montfort's death, until Louis VIII arrived.

"We defeated Montfort here, Father," Raymond VII said. "And we can defeat the King, as well."

"The *prince.* He's not a king yet!" Raymond VI replied scornfully. "I can't believe that King Phillip is waging war on me. We have been friends all of our lives.

"So be it! Bring me my sword," he commanded.

* * * * *

A few weeks later, Robierre rode through the gates of Laurac Castle, exhilarated. He could not believe what had happened. This time, it would be good news that he reported.

"Raymond won!" Robierre exclaimed, when he found the Countess. "The siege is over. The prince is marching his army back to Paris."

"What happened?" Blanche asked, surprised. "It's been only six weeks."

"Louis gave up. He didn't even build a trebuchet to break through the walls. Perhaps he is aware of the nine-month battle at Toulouse that cost Montfort his life. Perhaps he has no patience for a long siege." Robierre shrugged. "Who knows?"

"Why would he march back to Paris, when he is so close to victory?" Blanche asked, perplexed.

"A war with England? I don't know," Robierre replied.

"He'll be back. And stronger than before," stated Blanche.

* * * * *

As Blanche waited for the return of Louis VIII and his army, the summer of 1219 turned into a further liberation of Languedoc. Since Montfort's death in 1218, Languedoc had returned to a semblance of its past.

In September, Blanche decided that it was safe enough for Joanna to come home. She found Robierre, and discussed the matter with him.

"Robierre, where is Amaury's small band of Crusaders?"

"They are currently in Albige, Countess."

"If Joanna comes home, are they a threat to her?"

Robierre shook his head. "No, Countess. Amaury has a very small and incompetent army. And he hasn't wandered through Lauragaise since Prince Louis left for Paris."

"Do you think the Perfecti are safe in Lauragaise?" she asked, wanting to hear a further confirmation.

He nodded. "This summer I have seen Perfecti preaching in most of the towns and villages. Life has returned to the past. I'm sure that Joanna will be safe."

Blanche nodded, accepting his opinion. "Send word to Joanna that it is safe to come home."

Robierre bowed and left the room.

* * * * *

A few days later, Joanna walked to Laurac. She brought all of her belongings—which easily fit into a small bag—hoping to remain at the castle indefinitely.

She entered the castle in her long brown robe and sandals, set down her bag, and asked a servant for her mother's location.

"She is alone in the great room, my Lady."

As Joanna entered the great room, her mother sat majestically before her, clothed in a splendid frock of purple and blue. Blanche rose to greet her daughter, and Joanna smiled to herself, knowing that she was home.

"Mother, it is so good to see you," Joanna said, hugging her mother tightly. "Have you heard? Many of the Perfecti have left Montségur and returned home. It is safe at last!"

Blanche grinned. "Yes, it is safe. You can stay and live in the castle."

"Oh, that is wonderful! I can teach my girls at the Perfecti Women's Home. They must miss me."

Blanche smiled. "Yes, they need you. There are so few Perfecti left."

Joanna felt a pang of sadness for all of those they had lost.

"Did Gilbert remain?" Blanche asked.

"Yes, Montségur is his home now. I don't think he will ever leave. He has matured so much. He is now in charge of the monastery, and all of the Perfecti defer to him.

"He is a very good man," Blanche replied.

"Yes. I love him so much," Joanna answered. "Too bad we can never marry," she said wistfully.

* * * * *

The next day, Joanna walked to the Perfecti Women's Home. They had been waiting for her, and she was long overdue.

"Hello, girls," she said, entering the front door with a warm smile. "It has been far too long. I have missed all of you so much!"

"We missed you, too," replied one of the girls – actually now a young woman. "Where is Gilbert?"

"He is at Montségur. I have moved home to live with my mother again. So you will be seeing much more of me now."

One of the girls clapped her hands. "Oh, good!"

The rest of the girls came running when they heard that Perfecti Joanna had arrived, and all of the girls soon gathered around her to hug her and welcome her home.

And then, it was time for their training lesson. A stream of ubiquitous brown robes followed Joanna to the back room. After they each found a place to sit, one of the girls asked about the crusade.

"Perfecti Joanna, how long will there be peace in Languedoc?"

Joanna hesitated for a moment, as this was probably her least favorite topic. "The crusade was halted months ago," she said, "and I have not heard any rumors of it restarting. Hopefully, it will never start again.

"Let us enjoy our peace for now," she continued. "This is the happiest time of my life. I have waited years to be able to walk the streets of Laurac and serve God. Today, in all of Languedoc, the Perfecti are serving the people. It is a wonderful time."

"I want to serve, too," one of the girls pleaded.

"Yes, I want to be a Perfecti and serve God, as well," echoed another.

Joanna smiled. "Well then, let's work on it."

The small group of young ladies—they were no longer teenagers—all smiled eagerly, full of anticipation for what Joanna had to say today.

"Let's begin today with Mary Magdalene. She said that we should be able to telepathically talk to each other using the *nous*, even if we are not in the same room or the same village. She also said that this connection should allow us to communicate with those in God's Kingdom."

"You mean I can talk to my father, who was burned by the Crusaders?" asked one of the girls, in an animated voice.

"Yes, that is certainly possible," Joanna replied, "because you are still connected to his soul. If you pray to him, he will hear you. This is possible even if he has already incarnated, because only part of the soul incarnates. Another part always remains in God's Kingdom."

"What do you mean by a *part* of the soul?" the girl asked.

"When the body dies, the piece of our soul that was in that body returns to God's Kingdom. Once we arrive in Heaven, we either prepare to reincarnate into a new body, or we remain in God's Kingdom. It is taught that Perfecti do not reincarnate, but I still have some doubts about that."

"Our soul has parts?" another girl asked skeptically.

"Yes!" Joanna replied emphatically, slapping her knee and summarily dismissing the girl's doubts.

"Right now, in this room, each of us is a part of God's soul. That is how God's soul is split apart. In the same way, our soul can split into many parts. This is how Jesus can appear to many people at once. Each piece of our soul thinks that it is separate. But ultimately, all pieces come from the same source."

"Amazing!" a girl replied. "That means that, right now, a part of my soul could be enjoying God's Kingdom and talking to Jesus!"

Joanna nodded. "That is true."

"Do you believe that our soul is eternal?" another girl asked. "That everyone's destiny is to someday live forever in God's Kingdom?"

Joanna nodded. "Yes. That is what Jesus told Mary Magdalene."

"Everyone? All souls are eternal?" the same girl asked.

"You're missing the point," Joanna replied, with a chuckle. "Everyone *is* God. The question you are posing implies that each and every one is *separate* from God. That's an illusion. Thus, the behavior of an individual does not preclude them from being a manifestation of God."

"So, we're *really* God?" a girl asked incredulously.

"Yes. Our soul is part of God's soul, and finding that connection is life's quest. That is the Perfecti's mission—finding the *nous*. However, the illusion of the material world makes that mission difficult. By incarnating, we have exposed ourselves to a false reality.

"Moreover, we are searching for something that doesn't appear to exist—our true self. The material world can keep us blocked from finding the *nous*. If we focus on the material world and our ego, then we will never find it. The mind—the mischief-maker—blocks us from God.

"We can only find our link to God by using a silent, quiet mind. As Mary Magdalene states: 'Henceforth, I travel toward

Repose, where time rests in the Eternity of Time; I go now into Silence.'"[40]

"The quiet mind allows the heart to hear the *nous*," a girl said.

Joanna smiled. "Yes. By stilling the mind we open that gateway."

"And that is how God hears us?" the same girl asked.

"Yes," Joanna replied, "every word and every thought, and anyone at the other end of the channel can communicate with us. It is two-way communication."

"I don't hear anyone," a girl said.

"Oh, but you do," Joanna said. "Haven't you ever had a thought pop into your head that asked you to do something? For instance, when you are cooking, do you ever hear a voice tell you that it's done? Everyone hears voices all the time."

"But can't that voice be the ego?" a girl asked.

"Indeed. Good question. This is what makes becoming a Perfecti so difficult. We have to know the difference between the ego and the *nous*. The ego identifies with this world. That is the biggest difference. The ego would prefer that you burned your dinner, so that you became upset. The ego likes drama and could care less about your happiness. The more anxiety you have, the more the ego is in control. The ego is only concerned about one thing, its continued existence. Conversely, the voice from the *nous* is always trying to help you. That is the difference."

All of the girls nodded.

"Is there anyone that God rejects?" asked a girl, changing the subject.

"No," Joanna said. "This is impossible, because we are all part of God's soul. It would be the equivalent of God rejecting itself."

"Perfecti Joanna, if there is only God's soul, of which we are all a part, then aren't we all one big family?" asked one of the girls.

40 *Gospel of Mary Magdalene*, Jean-Yves Leloup, Inner Traditions, 2002, p. 16-17.

"Yes!" Joanna replied excitedly. "All of humanity is God's family, and we are all brothers and sisters. Actually, we are all the same, we are all God. Our soul *is* God. There is truly no separation between each of us. We are all one and the same.

"However, our earthly body disguises our connectedness. This is the reason for your daily prayers and daily meditations. They are used to re-connect you to God through the *nous*. It is the spirit that connects us to God, not our brain or earthly flesh.

"As Perfecti, we seek to connect more to spirit and less to our bodies. This is why we don't eat flesh, except for fish. This is why we remain celibate. This is why we take vows not to lie or steal or condemn. We do this to remain pure, and to open the gateway to the *nous*, because this is where God resides."

Joanna waited for someone to respond.

"I think I understand, Perfecti Joanna. The world is not where we find God or even Love. These are both found within, through our connection to spirit. The external world of matter only leads us astray, away from God. It is when we focus on the inner world that God manifests."

Joanna nodded, surprised by the clarity of the response. "Yes. That was beautifully explained. Your words were as eloquent as any Perfecti has ever spoken."

"I just realized something, Perfecti Joanna," said another girl. "To lie, steal, or condemn all require thought! Isn't this the mischief-maker that Mary Magdalene spoke of in her Gospel?"

Joanna smiled. "Indeed. It is an active mind that causes mischief. If you keep your mind quiet and focus on the inner world of spirit, then your connection to God will keep you saintly. Everyone has an inherently good soul. It is the mind and the material world that lead us astray. The soul is pure love, and that purity can be manifested into this lifetime. That is what Jesus and Mary Magdalene did—our Perfecti examples.

"A quiet the mind is the doorway to God?" asked one of the girls.

"Indeed," Joanna replied. "It is the basis of being a Perfecti. Only a quiet mind can coexist with God. This is what makes our relationship with God possible. A chattering, active mind can only keep you focused on the world of matter. This is not where God resides, but Satan."

"Yes, we know," a girl replied. "This world is of Satan."

"Is there any doubt?" Joanna asked. "Do you not see war, fear, hunger, poverty, murder, rape, inequity…"

"No, we do not doubt the world is of Satan," a girl interrupted. "If the world was of God, then it would be based on love, and there would be harmony."

Joanna nodded. "Exactly. This is the key to being a Perfecti. Do not be of this world. Keep your focus on your inner spirit. That is your link to God. If you will do this, you will have nothing to fear from the world."

"Can I ask a question, Perfecti Joanna?"

"Of course," Joanna said.

"Why did God create a world of Satan?" a girl asked.

"Oh, but he didn't," Joanna began. "God created nature and animals, but those are not of Satan. The evil that exists in the world is created by our own choices. We create society using our ego, the mischief-maker. Our ego's lead us astray and create the world of Satan."

"Perfecti Joanna, you make it sound nearly impossible to create a world without Satan," one of the girls said sadly.

"It's not impossible, but it is difficult," Joanna replied. "According to my mother, in many, many years, the Gnostics will come back and will create a world without Satan. They will create a world that is alignment with love. Perfecti Pierre told her that Mary Magdalene had a prophecy about this in her

Book of Love. It tells us that peace on earth will occur in another millennium."

"I wish it was now!" someone exclaimed.

The girls all laughed.

"There is a reason the world is of Satan," Joanna continued. "For instance, would all of you like to be like Mary Magdalene?"

Every girl in the room nodded.

"Well, that is your destiny, but this can happen only through the world of Satan. God created this world and gave us free will to make our own choices. Lifetime after lifetime, we use our free will and our choices to become like Jesus and Mary Magdalene. They had to endure exactly what we are enduring.

"The trials, the mischief of the mind, our fears, the temptations—all of it has a purpose. We have to endure hardship so that we will know, experientially, what is compassion, forgiveness, humanity, patience, or love.

"Satan's world has a definite purpose. It allows us to experience the kind of negativity that is not possible in God's Kingdom. From these experiences, our soul evolves and becomes more like God. All of us are growing spiritually. Like Jesus says, you will do greater things than I!"

"Perfecti Joanna, are you saying that the crusade is good for our souls? That we are learning from it?"

Joanna nodded, and then hesitated, anticipating their resistance. "I know that it sounds incredible, but it is true. Free will creates mischief, but it also allows our souls to evolve."

"Perfecti Joanna, do you mean that free will allows the Pope to send the Crusaders?"

"Yes. Free will allows people the ability to ignore God's love and follow Satan's evil ways."

"Perfecti Joanna, doesn't free will just make a mess of the world?"

"Well, sometimes it looks that way," laughed Joanna. "God knows that we are going to make mistakes, but God has infinite patience, and waits for our souls to evolve and grow with wisdom. He forgives all of our indiscretions, waiting for us to evolve. It might take more than a thousand lifetimes until we evolve as much as Jesus and Mary Magdalene. But eventually, everyone finds their way to God's Kingdom."

"Even evil souls like the Crusaders?" a girl asked.

"Remember, it is not the soul of the Crusader that is evil, but the body and the ego. It is the world of matter that leads one astray, not the soul. The soul is inviolate; it is eternally perfect; it is one with God. This is why we are to love our enemies. Their soul is as pristine as any soul. And never forget, they are our brothers and sisters in spirit. We are all one and we are all related."

"I'm sorry, Perfecti Joanna. I should know better than to condemn."

"Don't feel guilty," Joanna replied. "Instead, forgive yourself for your indiscretion, and recognize that you have just learned a lesson. By forgiving yourself, you will not need to learn that lesson again.

"Also, forgiving yourself is the same thing as loving yourself. This is a crucial step towards finding God. For, until we love ourselves, we won't believe that God loves us. Forgiveness opens the door to recognizing the incredible amount of love that God feels for us. Then you can begin to understand that God really forgives all of our indiscretions. No longer do we need to feel guilty, or even ask for forgiveness. All we have to do is forgive ourselves."

"Perfecti Joanna, you say not to feel guilty, but isn't guilt the same as our conscience telling us right from wrong?"

Joanna had to think this one over for a moment.

"I used to think guilt was my conscience, but now I know it is my ego tricking me. Guilt has no place in the heart of the soul. Guilt is simply the ego keeping us from our purity. The key to spiritual awareness is not guilt, but forgiveness.

"Forgiveness is the only way to learn the lesson. Otherwise, you are destined to repeat it. Everyone encounters guilt, and has regrets, but it is the lack of love for ourselves and for God that keeps us repeating the indiscretion. If you love yourself enough and love God enough, then an indiscretion is not possible."

A hand went up. "So, we should forgive the Crusaders or else our hatred will keep us from loving ourselves and God?"

"Exactly. All souls are evolving, even the Crusaders. We are all prodigal sons and daughters trying to find our way home."

"And the closer we get," Joanna added, "the bigger the smile on God's face. If you can imagine the smile on your mother's face after you have returned from a very long journey, imagine God's face after our long, long journey back home. It is a very warm welcome!"

Joanna got up. "Okay girls, it is time for you to go pray and meditate. Find your soul—for when you do, you will also find God."

CHAPTER FOURTEEN

Period of Respite

A few weeks later, Gilbert came to visit Joanna at Laurac Castle. He strode into the castle and met Joanna with a big smile, wearing his plain brown robe.

"Gilbert, you came to visit," Joanna said, rushing to give him a hug.

"I had to see what you were doing. I heard that you have been teaching the girls."

She nodded. "Why don't you come with me today? You can teach their lesson. They are really doing well. I think my job is almost done."

"I would be honored," he answered.

* * * * *

Later that day, they made their way to the Perfecti Women's Home.

"Girls, we are privileged to have Perfecti Gilbert with us again today. He is going to give you a special lesson."

The girls all sat quietly, as Gilbert began his discussion.

"Hello, girls. It is a pleasure to be here. Joanna has told me how well all of you have been doing. Soon, many of you will be receiving the *consolamentum*, and will become Perfecti. Today, I hope that this lesson is something that you can pass on to other aspiring Perfecti.

"The question that everyone has to ask themselves at some point in their lives is this: What is the unknown mystery of life? Where did we come from? Who created this world? What happens when we die? How we approach this unknown mystery determines our spirituality."

Gilbert held up two fingers.

"There are really only two ways to approach it. The first way is a spiritual quest to find the mystery. This is the way of the Gnostic. It is a quest to cross the barrier of the mystery and literally find the answer to these questions. For a Gnostic, this is an unyielding quest that is intense, passionate, and mystical. It leads to only one outcome, the discovery of God.

"Anyone who chooses the path of the Gnostic is transformed to a certain degree. They may not become enlightened and find the truth that they are one with God, but they will definitely find something that changes their awareness. At the very least, most will discover that God exists.

"The path of the Gnostic is an inner journey. Once you begin to look within, you will always find something. No longer will God be an idea or a belief, but a reality. You will literally *know* that God exists. Once this happens, the journey within becomes even more intense and passionate. The inner world becomes the real world, and the focus of your life. That is the way of the Gnostic. It is a path to purity, awareness, and mastery of the ego.

"The second way is an external path. This is the path of the material world. For example, this is the path of the Catholics. Instead of finding the truth within, the truth is given through Church dogma and the Bible. This leads to the blind acceptance of church beliefs, and involves living by *faith*.

"The external path is not only the path of the Catholics, but anyone who avoids the inner path. It is essentially a false path, because it can never lead to God, or show one the true meaning of life. Moreover, it will lead to confusion, conflict, fear, and a whole host of negative emotions.

"One of the biggest differences between a Gnostic and a non-Gnostic is the fear of death. A Gnostic knows that we are eternal, divine souls, and that we cannot die.

"Another difference is the concept of oneness. A Gnostic knows that God exists as one soul that encompasses everything, and that consciousness is what links everything and everyone together.

"Conversely, a non-Gnostic believes in separation. This separation inevitably leads to fear. For, if you believe that you are separate from God, then you are afraid of your destiny. It becomes a big unknown. The future becomes a terrifying event that is dependent on our choices and achievements. Thus, non-Gnostics believe in the illusion that each of us is on our own.

"Fear is actually a barrier between the seeker and God. Why? Because fear is the opposite of love. And, as any Gnostic knows, God *is* love."

"Okay, I have talked enough. Who has questions?"

"Perfecti, Gilbert, is the inner path a discovery of our true self?" asked a girl.

He nodded. "Yes. Jesus and Mary Magdalene taught us that God is within, and that God is only found with a quiet mind. This inner path leads to our true self, which is inherently good. If we can learn to focus on the inner path, we will be saints, just like Jesus and Mary Magdalene."

"We will be Perfecti," replied a girl, excitedly.

"Yes, you will be Perfecti. The spiritual quest to discover the mystery leads to nothing less than a transformation of consciousness. Our ego, our persona, is recognized for what it truly is, an illusion. We also discover that we are not only God, but one with everything. This awareness leads us to stop judging other people and to allow them their own journey. Everyone will find God in their own way, and it can be a very long journey."

"Perfecti, Gilbert, should we help them to find God, since we know the way?"

He shook his head. "Only if we are asked. It is up to them to decide if they are going to pursue an inner path in this lifetime. Until someone has found the inner path on their own, there is nothing you can do. The inner path is something to which people are drawn. It is not an accident, but a destiny. If someone is supposed to begin an inner journey to God, then they will. It is not for us to think that we know when it is their time."

The young ladies all nodded in understanding.

"Perfecti Gilbert, is this because it can take thousands of lifetimes to find God?"

He nodded. "Yes. How are we to know that this is the lifetime that they are ready to begin their inner journey? Only they can know that."

"Perfecti Gilbert, I am using the inner path, but I have not yet found God. Can you explain what I am looking for?"

Gilbert smiled at her sincerity, and paused for a few seconds of quiet reflection.

"Well, I think that all of you have found God, or else you would not be here today. Perhaps what you have not yet found is absolute proof. Don't worry, that will come. All you need to do is keep listening to that inner voice.

"God speaks in a still, small voice that comes from deep inside your spirit—from the *nous*. It can seem like you are thinking your own thoughts. And yet, the information is not coming from your own mind. Sometimes God will answer your questions. Other times, God may give you information about a situation that you could not possibly know about.

"Are you familiar with experiencing a revelation or an epiphany? One of those moments when the light suddenly dawns? When you suddenly realize something clearly that has been hidden? That is God speaking to you.

"Have you ever prayed for an answer, and then had several people start giving it to you, from several different and unconnected sources, without you even having to mention what you need? That is also God speaking to you, through others.

"The scriptures and ancient knowledge can help guide you, and they can provide revelations. Also, meditation and an inner focus can make it much easier to hear God's voice.

"Remember to be vigilant regarding the material world and the ego, as both will get in your way and distract you from your path. Sometimes, it can be very hard to discard ego, and listen to that quiet voice within.

"Does everybody understand what I am talking about?"

Gilbert looked around, and heads were nodding everywhere, so he decided that they had finally understood the message.

As usual, Joanna was pleased with how simply Gilbert was able to communicate with the girls and get his point across.

"Perfecti Gilbert," a girl asked. "I have heard that Jesus studied in the East. What did they teach him?"

Gilbert smiled. "Ah, yes, this is a good question. A mystic of the East and a Gnostic of the West are essentially the same. A mystic is also on an inner journey to finding God. They meditate far more than we do, but their objectives are the same. They are trying to connect to spirit in a higher dimension.

"Some mystics are so connected to the spiritual realm that they can perform miracles, such as levitating or manifesting something out of nothing. Jesus learned some of these mystical ways, which he used for his miracles."

"Perfecti Gilbert, are mystics also saints?"

He nodded. "Sure, if you met a mystic, you would consider him saintly. Those who are strongly connected to the inner self are saintly. Almost everyone who finds God is incredibly saintly.

Once you find God, you become God-like, and God is inherently loving and good.

"Another example would be Jesus and Mary Magdalene. They were loving, kind, generous, allowing, compassionate, and humane. They are the example that we are trying to emulate."

Joanna got up. "Okay girls, that is enough for today. It is time for you to go pray and meditate."

Each one of the girls thanked Gilbert personally, as they left the room.

* * * * *

Three years passed without the resumption of the crusade. It was now July, 1222. It seemed like life in Languedoc had reverted to the past. Perfecti preached in public, and freely walked the streets of the towns and villages. Joanna continued to live with her mother and teach the girls at the Perfecti Women's Home.

Unfortunately, this brief respite was destined to end. Blanche waited uneasily for the Crusaders to return. She knew that one day a courier would arrive with the news that she had nervously anticipated.

Finally that day arrived, and Robierre was summoned to the castle gates. At first, when he heard the news, he was not sure of its significance. It seemed so long ago that the Crusaders had marched through Lauragaise. As he walked towards the castle to find the Countess, he wondered if this could bring the dreaded Crusaders back.

"Countess," Robierre said, finding her outside in the garden, "Raymond VI has succumbed to old age. He died last night in his sleep."

Blanche gasped, as she had been praying that he would hang onto life for a few more years. "This is a sad day," she said. "I fear the crusade is going to come back. Years ago, the Pope declared that Raymond VII could not inherit his father's land. So today, there are no rightful owners of Languedoc. This surely will create another war."

"Countess, there are rumors that Raymond VII is going to agree to terms with the Pope, so that he can inherit his father's land."

Blanche hesitated. "If that happens, then surely the Crusaders will return to kill the Perfecti. Should I send Joanna back to Montségur?"

"Not yet, my lady. There will be ample warning."

Blanche nodded in agreement. She did not want to see her daughter leave any sooner than necessary.

* * * * *

A whole year went by. It was now July, 1223. During the past year, Raymond VII had negotiated with the Pope and King Phillip Augustus to inherit his father's land. The negotiations had been tedious, and were still not resolved.

A courier came to the gates of Château Narbonnais, and Antoine was summoned. After hearing the news, he walked dejectedly to find young Raymond. He knew that the Count would not like the news.

He found him in the great room, dressed in his embroidered regalia.

"Yes, Antoine?"

"My Lord, King Phillip Augustus has died."

Raymond VII looked at Antoine with sudden fear in his eyes. "No! No! No!"

He began pacing the floor nervously—like a wild man possessed.

"Now we cannot complete our negotiations! Prince Louis will now be king! And he will certainly march on Languedoc. My father and I embarrassed him twice in the war. He will want his revenge!"

"I fear you are right, my Lord. We may have to defend Toulouse."

"Send emissaries to Comminges and Foix. See if they will help."

* * * * *

Several months passed. It was now January, 1224, and Louis VIII had assumed the throne. Young Raymond's instincts were correct. Shortly after Raymond VI had died, King Louis VIII discontinued the negotiations to resolve Raymond's inheritance. Instead, he began negotiations with the Pope to lead a new crusade. His desire to add all of Languedoc to his empire was evident.

A new message was sent to Château Narbonnais. Antoine grinned when he heard the news, and he was sure that the Lord would be pleased. Walking to the castle, he wondered if this was truly a signal of final peace for the region.

He found young Raymond in the great room. He entered the room and stood at attention.

"Yes, Antoine."

"My Lord, King Louis VIII made an offer to lead the crusade and was turned down by Pope Honorius. In fact, the Pope has officially cancelled the crusade. Amaury is disbanding his army and returning home to his family's estate in Rambouillet. Also, the sixteen-year-old son of Raymond-Roger Trencavel has finally been given his father's titles of Count of Bèziers and Carcassonne. Languedoc has returned to 1209!"

Raymond VII hesitated. "No, Antoine, it has not. My father's lands still have not been given to me. I live as an outlaw in the eyes of the Pope and perhaps King Louis VIII, as well. The Counts of Foix and Comminges are in the same position as myself. Legally, our lands have been usurped."

"My Lord, this might finally be the end of the crusade." Antoine grinned. "You will simply need to continue your negotiations with Pope Honorius. It was the Papacy who took your father's land."

Raymond nodded. "Yes, but I also need to negotiate with the King. I have two powerful enemies—either of which can mount an army larger than mine. Peace can never be assured until I have my father's land and terms have been agreed to by the Pope and the King."

Antoine was still optimistic. "Your father did all that he could to protect the Perfecti and our way of life. He battled Montfort for nine years from 1209 until 1218, and watched as thousands of Perfecti were burned. Now you can achieve the final victory that he sought."

"I will try, but my enemies are strong. I would love to save God's apostles, the Perfecti, but only time will tell."

Antoine bowed and left the room.

* * * * *

Two more years passed. It was now June, 1226. Young Raymond was no longer young. He was nearing his thirtieth birthday. His negotiations had faltered, time and time again, with the Pope and the King. The Pope was stubbornly refusing to give Raymond his father's land.

Even though Pope Honorius had halted the crusade, he still wanted to eliminate the Cathars. And they were still strong in the Lauragaise region, even though they had nearly been eliminated in the rest of Languedoc.

Raymond and his father had been a persistent aggravation for the last two Popes. In fact, they were the only reason that the Cathars still existed. So the Pope would simply not allow Raymond to regain a position of strength in Lauragaise.

A courier rode to Château Narbonnais and Antoine was summoned. But this time, it was dreadful news. Antoine had witnessed the entire crusade, and had hoped that it was over. But he knew now that his hope had been misguided.

He listened to the news stoically, and then proceeded to the castle to inform the Count. He found him in the great room.

"Yes, Antoine?"

"My Lord, Louis VIII is marching on Avignon. His army is very large. More than two thousand men."

Raymond nodded, and sighed deeply. "I knew that this was coming when he refused to negotiate with me. He wants my land. He has been negotiating with the Pope for two years to lead the crusade."

"Do you want me to go to Avignon?"

"No, we need to prepare to defend Toulouse. Go to Comminges and Foix. We will need their armies. King Louis will come here next."

* * * * *

Four months later, a courier brought news to Laurac. Like Antoine, Robierre listened stoically to more bad news. The crusade had resumed, and it was not going well for their side.

Robierre walked towards the castle with mixed emotions. He had seen the crusade stop and start so many times that he was not sure of the outcome. Every time it appeared that the Crusaders had the upper hand, the tide would turn. But he was still terrified, and he knew that their luck had to eventually run out against such powerful enemies.

He found the Countess outside in the garden, playing with her grandchildren. When she saw him approach, her joyful exuberance was replaced with a dark sense of foreboding. She quickly walked away from her grandchildren, leaving them with a servant, and moved toward Robierre, holding her gown above the grass as she walked.

"Do you bring news of Avignon?" Blanche asked.

Robierre nodded. "Countess, Avignon has finally surrendered. King Louis' army was big enough to surround the town. They didn't have a chance."

"Were any Perfecti burned?"

"No, Countess. I don't think Louis VIII is after the Perfecti. He came for the land. He arrested a hundred of the town's leaders, and laid claim to the town as his own."

Blanche took a deep breath, as she gazed down at Laurac off in the distance and down in the valley. "Interesting. If he rules the land, he will allow the Pope to find the remaining Perfecti and eliminate the Cathars."

"Also, Countess, Avignon is part of Raymond's land. Thus, he has declared war on Raymond. I fear he will attack Toulouse next."

Blanche nodded, in quiet resignation, but her eyes welled up with tears. "I must send Joanna back to Montségur now. It's not fair. She has been home for seven years!"

"I know," Robierre said. "She has been happy here."

Blanche gathered her composure, and turned her attention back to the grim situation at hand. "Go see Raymond VII at Château Narbonnais, and see if he needs our help."

Robierre bowed and walked away.

CHAPTER FIFTEEN

The Crusade is Over—1229

Two months later, in November 1226, a miracle happened. The Cathars' luck had not yet run out.

Antoine rode through the gates at Château Narbonnais with a few of his fellow knights. After he dismounted and handed the reigns to a servant, he immediately headed into the castle. For a man of his age, he walked with a very spry step on this day.

He went straight to the great room, still wearing his battle clothing, and found Raymond VII sitting in his majestic chair, dressed in all his regalia.

"Hello, Antoine. What news do you bring?" Raymond asked.

"My Lord! King Louis VIII has died of dysentery!"

Raymond's jaw dropped and his mouth gaped open.

"And his army?" he finally spurted.

"Most of the Royal Army is returning to Paris," said Antoine. A small contingent of five hundred knights were left, under the command of Humbert of Beaujeu, to defend what Louis has captured."

A new light of hope entered Raymond's eyes, as he nodded. "Yes, they have to defend the Monarchy. The King's son, Prince Louis IX, is only twelve-years-old. The French Monarchy is vulnerable with such a young king."

"My Lord, do you think they will return?"

Raymond contemplated. "Yes, but I don't know when. After Avignon, King Louis marched through the Carcassonne region and was welcomed by the citizens without resistance. He placed his seneschals in charge of the towns. Surely, this will give the Monarchy confidence to come back and claim all of Languedoc."

"I agree, my Lord. Now that the Monarchy has claimed Avignon and parts of Carcassonne, it is simply a matter of time before they claim all of Languedoc."

Raymond hesitated to reply. "Antoine, now that Louis VIII is finally gone, do you think I should negotiate terms with the Monarchy?"

Antoine quickly nodded. "My Lord, the Counts of Foix and Comminges have already surrendered to King Louis VIII. And I don't think we can defend Toulouse if the Royal Army comes back."

Raymond reflected for a moment. "I agree. It is time to negotiate terms. I would be a fool to fight to the death defending Toulouse. I hope that my father can forgive me for abandoning the Cathars. I'm afraid that they are doomed."

Antoine closed his eyes and bowed his head at this distressing turn of events. Then he turned and quickly left the room.

* * * * *

In the spring of 1227, Blanche sent for her daughter at Montségur to come home and live in the castle. The crusade had been halted since King Louis VIII's death, and it was safe again for Perfecti in Lauragaise.

When Joanna returned and entered the castle, she was greeted by her mother with elation. Little did either of them realize that, in one year, both would be relegated to Montségur. This would be their last time to live in the enchantment of Laurac Castle.

* * * * *

A few days after her return, Joanna walked to the Perfecti Women's Home to teach her girls. All of them were now past thirty years of age, but the same group still attended her lessons. When she walked through the door with her ever-present smile and enthusiasm, the women gave her a joyous welcome.

"Today we are going to do something special," Joanna said. "I saw a Dominican on my way here. All of you, get ready. We are going to approach him, and I am going to debate him."

The women had a sudden look of horror in their eyes. Ever since the crusade had begun, they rarely went outside, and this seemed incredibly risky to them.

"Won't he report us to the Catholic Bishop?" one of the women asked fearfully.

"Maybe. But isn't it likely that the Catholic Bishop already knows about you?"

Joanna paused, as she could see that distress was on everyone's face.

"This Perfecti Women's Home is not a secret to the people of Laurac," she said convincingly. "Why should we live in fear? This is our town, not the Catholics'. Let us confront the Dominican, and show the people that the Perfecti are still the apostles of Laurac."

"All of you, get ready," Joanna continued, with a louder voice. "I will not have my students living in fear. You are immortal divine beings! Now, hurry up!"

The women were not as courageous as Joanna. However, none of them protested any further, as they solemnly got their things together for a short walk into town.

Joanna led the way in a sea of brown robes. They all headed for the town square where Joanna had surveyed the Dominican. As they approached, she could see that he was still there, talking to a group of people.

Joanna approached and smiled at him. "Why do you confuse our citizens?" she asked the Dominican.

The Dominican was startled that a female Perfecti had approached him, and hardly knew how to respond. "I only tell them the word of God."

People around the square quickly surrounded them. There were now at least fifty people listening to the confrontation between Joanna and the Dominican.

"But you do not tell them that *they* are God. Instead, you frighten them into believing that God will judge their fate. On the one hand, you say that God is a loving God. On the other, you say that God's wrath will be felt by the non-believers, and that Hell awaits them. That is not true, and you are merely confusing them."

The Dominican held up his Bible as an answer, "Oh, but it is true! Only by the Son—Jesus—can one have salvation."

"No one needs salvation," Joanna replied. "We are already eternal, divine beings. What one needs is enlightenment, the knowledge that we *are* God. What that scripture is trying to tell you is that Jesus was a Gnostic, and that his knowledge of his own divinity is what gave him enlightenment. We, too, can achieve knowledge of our divinity, and this will lead to our enlightenment, our destiny to live in God's Kingdom. Faith alone does not give one enlightenment, but knowledge—Gnosis—does."

The Dominican shook his head in disgust. "And how do you find this Gnosis? You search and search and you find nothing. Salvation is found in the Church, through the sacraments, and the love of God and his son, Jesus."

Joanna grinned. "The Catholic Church will not lead one to enlightenment, not in this lifetime. Maybe in the next, but so will any path. All roads will eventually lead one to look within and find the *nous*. Your promise of salvation after this lifetime—

eternal residence in God's Kingdom—is not correct. Everyone who comes to your church will reincarnate. They will be born again and again until they are enlightened."

The Dominican had heard enough. He was now angry. "Your beliefs are heresy! You should be burned!"

The crowd did not react to his call for damnation.

Joanna stood stoically. "I can see that you do not want to debate. You have your own Church dogma, and everything else is considered heresy. I have no problem allowing you your religion, but you will not allow me mine. So be it. Good day."

Joanna turned and proceeded to walk back to the Women's Home, with the women following behind her. The confrontation revealed the schism that existed between the Cathars and the Catholics. The women and spectators had gotten a firsthand look at the intolerance of the day.

* * * * *

Later that year, in 1227, Pope Honorius III died. It was a bad omen. The new Pope, Gregory IX, inherited the unresolved Albigensian Crusade that dated back to 1209. It was inevitable that he would attempt a resolution for the Cathar problem.

In the summer of 1228, Pope Gregory made his decision. A courier arrived at Laurac Castle and informed Robierre.

He was shaken by the news. "Why now?" he thought ruefully. "Why can't they leave us alone?" It had been nearly a decade since Raymond VI had defeated Montfort—and two whole years since King Louis VIII had died leading the crusade.

He found Blanche and her daughter together in the great room. Blanche sat serenely in one of her beautiful gowns.

Blanche and Joanna had spent most of the past year together. Blanche rarely meditated, but she was still a Gnostic, like her daughter. And they often talked for hours on end about spirituality and ancient scriptures.

When Robierre entered, neither of them noticed his dour look. His elderly age was now showing, and he often looked tired.

Blanche smiled. "What is it, Robierre?"

Robierre sighed wearily. "The new Pope, Gregory IX, has called for the crusade to resume."

A chilling terror came over Blanche, and her face reflected her horror. "No!" she cried. She knew that this was, most likely, the end of the Cathars. Like Pierre had told her, their time would run out.

Everyone was silent as Blanche helplessly anticipated their fate. Joanna was the least affected. She sat there calmly, waiting for her mother to speak.

Blanche looked at Joanna. "You must return to Montségur. It is no longer safe in Laurac."

But Joanna was not anxious to return. "Mother, let me stay for a while longer," she pleaded. "Humbert has not brought his Royal Troops to Lauragaise. He has remained in Carcassonne and the Rhône Valley. His army isn't big enough to confront Raymond VII."

Blanche was adamant and would not give in. "Now that the crusade is to be resumed, his army could be reinforced any day and march into Lauragaise. It is simply not safe, Joanna."

Joanna did not wish to argue with her mother, especially since she could see the determination in her eyes. "Okay, Mother," she said peacefully. "I will return tomorrow. I'm sure Gilbert would like to see me." She rose and went to find her brother, nieces and nephews. It would be a sad goodbye for her, not knowing if she would ever be coming back. She knew full well the peril that she faced.

"Robierre," Blanche called out, "send someone to see Raymond VII. Find out his plans."

Robierre bowed and left.

* * * * *

A few months later, in 1229, the war was over. The Albigensian Crusade would never resume. However, that was *not* good news for the Cathars.

Robierre received the news from the courier at the gate and accepted it stoically. As he turned toward the castle to find Blanche, he was shattered. When he found her in the great room, he could not even look at her. Instead, he closed his eyes and then looked down at the floor.

Blanche saw him and was greatly surprised by his behavior. "What is it, Robierre?" she asked tentatively.

"Countess," Robierre said softly, "Raymond VII has accepted terms. Languedoc is now in the hands of the King. It is over. We have lost."

Blanche was stunned. "But the crusade never even resumed. Why would he give up so easily?"

"I don't know, Countess. Perhaps he didn't think he could defend Toulouse, and instead chose to save the people."

"Except the Perfecti! They will now all be killed!" Blanche said angrily, knowing that her daughter's life was in danger.

Robierre did not reply. He continued to stare at the floor.

"Tell me about the terms?" Blanche asked, her anger quickly subsiding into melancholy.

"They are very bad, Countess," he answered, looking up again. All of the eastern provinces, including the Rhône Valley are immediately annexed to the French Crown. All of Raymond's remaining properties are to be inherited by the King's brother, who has been betrothed to Joan, Raymond VII's only child."

Blanche stared back at him in shock. "Joan is only nine-years-old! This means that all of Raymond's land will be inherited by the Monarchy."

"Yes, Countess. All of Languedoc is now in the hands of the Monarchy. Raymond is now powerless without an army. He will live out his final days at Château Narbonnais, but then it, too, reverts to the Monarchy.

"After the agreement was signed in Paris, Joan was taken to live with the Royal Family. They're calling it the Treaty of Paris."[41]

Blanche shook her head. "This is terrible. We lose the war without even a battle! The Albigensian Crusade is over, but all of the Perfecti are going to be killed."

Robierre hesitated to answer. "I fear you are right, Countess. The Papacy finally has the backing of the secular powers to root out the Perfecti. The holy ones can no longer be protected by the nobles."

"How many Perfecti are left, Robierre?"

"Perhaps a thousand, possibly two thousand. It's hard to say, since so many are in hiding. It won't be long before they are all gone."

Tears streamed down Blanche's face, and she held her handkerchief over her mouth, while sobbing. Robierre just stood by silently, not showing his own emotions.

After a good ten minutes had passed, a grief stricken Blanche heaved a huge sigh of resignation and wiped her eyes. "I knew that this day would come," she said sadly.

* * * * *

The Catholics now controlled all of Languedoc. Shortly after Raymond VII signed the Treaty of Paris, the local bishops began to focus on the persecution of heresy. The Cathars were doomed, even though it would take decades to hunt them all down.

41 Raymond VII signed the Treaty of Paris April 12, 1229 in front of the Notre Dame Cathedral, which was under construction. He agreed to fight the Cathar heresy, to return all Church property, to demolish the defenses of Toulouse, and to turn over all his castles, as well as pay damages. This marked the end of independence in Languedoc. A few months later, the Inquisition was established in Languedoc.

The expected edict arrived by courier. It hurt when Robierre heard the development, but it was not a surprise. He nodded and headed for the castle.

When Blanche saw the look on his face, she knew that the Catholics were finally coming for the last of the Perfecti. She nodded at him to speak.

"Countess, a council of Catholic bishops has appointed an inquirer in each parish in Narbonne. These inquirers are to find the heretics and eliminate them. They have begun their Inquisition."

Blanche sighed. "Very well. We knew it was coming."

Robierre looked at Blanche while feeling extreme sadness. He was finding it difficult not to cry. After all of these years and now it had come to this.

"I'm going to Montségur to live with Joanna," Blanche said sadly, "and I will take the women from the Perfecti Women's Home with me."

Robierre nodded solemnly, knowing that they would all likely die soon at the hands of the Catholics.

"I will leave my son, Jean, in charge of the castle," she continued. "You will stay and counsel him."

Robierre bowed and, without looking up, said, "Yes, Countess, as you wish. But I will visit you."

Blanche tried smile at his thoughtfulness, but there was too much pain to bare. "Thank you, Robierre. I would like that."

Chapter Sixteen

Montségur

Robierre did not visit for nearly a year. As he hiked to the top of Montségur, he realized that he could not make this climb for too many more years. His old body rebelled with every step, forcing him to frequently stop and rest. Finally, he saw the tall gates and got his second wind.

The gates were only opened a few feet, and when he entered, no one noticed. He was surprised by all the activity inside. There were more than a hundred Perfecti wearing their ubiquitous brown robes, along with numerous knights. Montségur had turned into a stronghold of resistance. People had been living here since the beginning of the crusade, yet this was the first time he had ever visited.

He walked up to the nearest Perfecti and asked for Blanche, the Countess of Laurac.

The Perfecti started walking, and waved him along. "This way," he said.

Robierre followed.

"You are new here," the Perfecti said, with a smile.

"Yes, Perfecti. This is my first visit."

"I can see from your clothing that you are a knight. Did you fight for the resistance?"

"Since the beginning, Perfecti."

"What is your name?" the Perfecti asked, continuing to walk toward the monastery.

"Robierre. I have been with the Countess since I was young."

"Why don't you stay and help us defend the fortress? We could always use one more knight."

Robierre smiled. "I'm too old for fighting now. Besides, the Countess wants me in Laurac."

The thought of defending Montségur against the Royal Army sent chills through Robierre's body. He knew that they would all die.

"Very well," the Perfecti replied. "At least stay for supper and spend the night. We would be honored to have you here. You have defended us with great courage for many years."

Robierre nodded. "Thank you for the invitation."

"You are welcome, Robierre," the Perfecti said, walking into the monastery.

Robierre followed the Perfecti as they traveled down a long stone hallway that was lit by lanterns. At the end of the hallway, they entered the great room. There, at one end of the room, was Blanche, sitting by herself.

The Perfecti stopped and pointed to her with his right arm and his palm up. His grin was genuine.

"Thank you, Perfecti," Robierre said, not returning the grin.

The Perfecti nodded, then turned and left.

As Robierre approached her, he was stricken by the dire situation before him. She still looked lovely, in one of her pale blue dresses. But it was almost as if she was imprisoned, and this is where she would spend her final days. He wanted to get her out of there and bring her home. But he knew that she wouldn't leave.

"Robierre," Blanche said warmly, forcing herself to grin, "it is so good to see you."

Robierre bowed. "Countess."

"What news do you bring?" Blanche asked, her former vitality no longer present.

Robierre had to hold back his emotions at her plight.

"Countess, the Perfecti continue to walk the streets and preach openly throughout Languedoc. However, it is becoming less frequent, and there have been persecutions. In Toulouse, the Bishop found nineteen Perfecti worshipping, and he burned them all."

Blanche forced another grin. "It's good to know that they persevere."

Robierre nodded. "In Lauragaise, the people are not cooperating with the bishops and inquisitors. There are many Perfecti being protected. Yesterday, I saw a Perfecti preaching in public in Laurac. They are very brave."

"That's good news," Blanche said quietly. She was no longer able to grin, as she stared vacantly at the nearest wall. All she could think about were Pierre's prophetic words that the Perfecti were doomed.

* * * * *

Nearly three years passed before Robierre made another trip to Montségur. This last trip was in 1234.

Robierre was now in his sixties, and an old man. The journey up the steep hill was not easy, but he was determined to see the Countess one more time, and to give her some new information.

He knew that it was his duty, but his determination stemmed from the fact that he loved the Countess. She had always been kind and generous to him, and treated him like family. And now he wanted to say goodbye. He knew that she would never leave Montségur alive.

Entering the gates, there was no change from before. It was lively, with scores of people in the courtyard. He headed for the monastery and the great room. He knew the Countess was a habitual person and, most likely, was in the same place as before.

Entering the great room through the long hall, he spotted the Countess sitting alone. These days, she no longer looked like a Countess. He recognized the same pale blue gown that he had seen her wear last time, but now it was threadbare, tattered and dirty. Her hair was a matted mess.

At first glance, he was angry that this had befallen her. But then his emotions turned to sadness, as he recognized the reality of the situation.

He approached her and grinned warmly.

"Robierre," Blanche said softly, smiling. "It is so good to see you."

Her former vitality was nearly gone, but at least she seemed to be at peace. Robierre sat down across from her.

"Countess, I'm sorry, but I bring more bad news," Robierre said dejectedly.

"It's okay, Robierre," Blanche replied softly. "I've been expecting it. What news do you bring?"

"Pope Gregory IX has expanded the Inquisition in Languedoc. It is now well organized. They are methodically hunting down all of the Perfecti and their supporters. He sent two Dominicans from Rome, Pierre Seilha and Guillaume Arnaud, to lead it.[42]

"They have been given extraordinary powers. Anyone suspected of being a heretic, or a supporter of a heretic, can be arrested, and their possessions confiscated. Nobles can even lose their titles. Hundreds of people have already been killed."

Blanche hesitated, wondering about the safety of Jean and her castle. "Tell me about their methods?" she said softly.

"The inquisitors arrest suspects that have been identified by local spies as either Perfecti or Cathar supporters. Then

42 This is where the Holy Inquisition began, but few people are aware of this fact, since it is not taught in schools.

they question the suspects. From what I hear, there has been no physical torture. However, the inquisitors are the judge and jury, and there are no public trials. Suspects do not get a lawyer. They are presumed guilty, and must defend themselves from accusations. Once charged, suspects have to prove their innocence. If they remain silent or judged guilty, they are killed."

Blanche shuddered.

Robierre continued. "The two Dominicans, Seilha and Guillaume, are currently in Moissac. Soon they will be in Lauragaise. I've been told that they have already killed more than 2,000 people. Many of them were prominent citizens who supported the Perfecti."

"That is what I feared," Blanche said softly. "The only way to eliminate the Perfecti is to also eliminate their supporters."

Robierre hesitated, not sure how clearly the Countess understood what she had just said. "Countess, that would include thousands of people in Lauragaise."

The Countess suddenly looked at Robierre with a spark of her former vitality. "I know, Robierre," she said in a patronizing tone. "It won't be an easy task for this Inquisition. It will take years."

Robierre realized that she did, indeed, understand. Every day, more and more people would be burned, until the remaining Perfecti and all of their supporters were gone. It was a true holocaust, being performed by the Catholic Church, merely to eliminate their competition.

Blanche and Robierre had held many discussions, over the years, about the end of the Cathars in Languedoc. And now, Blanche hoped that history would record all of this, so that, one day in the future, the Cathars could rise again … that one day, the Perfecti would walk the earth freely again. It was all she thought about.

"We lost, Countess," Robierre said sadly.

She grinned warmly. "Maybe not. There is always the future, Robierre. There will be more Cathars in the times ahead."

He remembered what Pierre had told the Countess about the end times, and nodded to her in agreement. Then a small silence ensued, as they both sat in quiet reflection.

Robierre gazed upon her lovely face, smiling in the midst of all this adversity, and thought about how wonderful it had been to see Blanche for one last time. However, his duty had been completed, and he reluctantly turned his thoughts to departing. He knew that she had missed his company, and he dreaded having to tell her that he was not coming back again. But finally, he broke the silence.

"I fear that this is our final goodbye, Countess," he said weakly, averting her eyes. I am getting too old to come back here again."

As he had feared, the Countess was taken aback by his statement. And one more loss just seemed too much for her to bear. As the initial shock subsided, she broke down and started crying. "Oh, Robierre, I will miss you," she sobbed uncontrollably. "Can I at least hug you to say goodbye?"

Robierre smiled at her gracefully and nodded, his eyes welling up with tears of sympathy. She rose gingerly, and he walked to meet her. They had known each other for nearly forty years, but had never touched.

Then she opened her arms, and he embraced her. The love they felt for each other was painfully emotional. It was not just friendship. She felt more like a dear sister to him. Robierre cried, on her shoulder, for the first time since he was a child.

"I will miss you, Countess," Robierre said, after they had finished embracing, and had looked into each other's tear-drenched faces.

"You have been my most loyal friend, Robierre. Thank you. Take care of Jean and my family."

"I will, my Lady."

He turned to leave, and, after a few steps, he looked back. She was still standing there, watching him walk away. He only glanced at her, but it was one of the hardest things he had ever done. He knew that this was not the outcome that she had wanted. And the thought of her impending death hurt him far more than any battle wound ever could.

* * * * *

On the other side of the monastery, Joanna was teaching her girls from Laurac, all of whom were now in their thirties and forties.

"Perfecti Joanna, I've been reading Luke. I was wondering if these two scriptures are related. The first is Luke 6:40: Everyone, when his training is complete, will reach his teachers level. The second is Luke 11:52. Woe to you teachers of the law, for you took away the keys to Gnosis. You do not enter in yourselves, and you obstruct those who want to enter."

"Yes, they're related," Joanna replied. "The first identifies the quest of enlightenment. The truth is that everyone is in training. Everyone is searching for the path back to God. However, only the Gnostic acknowledges their spiritual quest as a training exercise. For, the Gnostic knows that once their quest is complete, that they, too, will be enlightened, just like Jesus and Mary Magdalene.

"The second scripture is an admonition to Rabbis in the Old Testament for not teaching the way of Gnosis. This scripture would also apply to the Catholics of today."

"Will we all reach enlightenment?" one of her students asked.

Joanna nodded.

"To answer that question, I have to mention Sophia, the Goddess of Wisdom. She is an archetype, a symbol. And she represents the keys to Gnosis, which is the wisdom that is necessary to attaining enlightenment. These keys are not found in a scroll or a book. They are found through inquiry, through the contemplation of spiritual philosophy.

"Enlightenment is attained through spiritual wisdom, which is represented by Sophia, and also by Mary Magdalene. Obtaining this wisdom does not occur by osmosis, but by deliberate intent and inquiry. The outcome of this journey is nothing less than the attainment of unlimited knowledge and wisdom.

"Sophia is Christ's feminine counterpart, and her wisdom can be represented as Mary Magdalene. Everyone can use the wisdom of Sophia to become one with Christ. But finding her wisdom through Gnosis is not an easy journey. Although, it is worth the effort, for the outcome of Gnosis is enlightenment, the awareness that we are one with God, and that our true identity is God's consciousness.

"Mary Magdalene used her love of Jesus to find the *nous,* and her wisdom to understand Gnosis, which can be literally translated as to *know* God. With her enlightenment, Mary Magdalene and Jesus became *one,* and this is known as the mystical marriage. Together, they represent the ultimate level of spiritual awareness: a blending and balancing of the masculine and the feminine. While Catholics and Gnostics both revere Jesus, only Gnostics also understand the significance of Mary Magdalene. Their combined energy represents the ultimate enlightenment."

There was a silence as the women contemplated, then one of the students raised her hand.

"Is this the same thing that Hermes said, that 'the goal of Gnosis is to become God?'"[43]

Joanna nodded. "Yes. Understanding the *nous* through contemplation and inquiry is a journey to becoming aware

43 Poimandres, Hermes Trismegistus, p. 573.

that we are God. More than that, it is literally tapping into the intelligence of God."

Joanna continued. "Hermes also said this, 'That in you which sees and hears is the Logos of the Lord. It is the Consciousness of God the Father.'[44] Could anything be clearer? His use of the word Logos, is the same thing as the *nous*."

"Perfecti Joanna, since this awareness is difficult to attain and usually takes many lifetimes, what are the signs that we are getting close to Gnosis?"

"Excellent question," Joanna replied. "The answer is that love will become paramount in your life. You will love yourself, God, and humanity to such an extent that all of your thoughts and actions will be in alignment with love. The five rules of love that Mary Magdalene wrote in The Book of Love come to mind:

1. Love God through devotion and service.
2. Love yourself because you are God.
3. Love your neighbors because they are you.
4. Love everyone because we are one.
5. Love humanity because we are family.

"Once you master these, her five rules of living become easy:

1. Be gentle and compassionate.
2. Be positive and passionate.
3. Be in allowance and acceptance.
4. Be content and grateful.
5. Be present, with a quiet mind.

"If you live by these rules, then you will live in bliss. Life on earth will become more dreamlike and less real. There will be more laughing and less crying; more tolerance and less judgment. But more than anything else, there will be more love and less fear."

44 Poimandres, Hermes Trismegistus, p. 195.

Joanna smiled. "Are there any other questions?"

Another hand went up. "I've been reading the Clement of Alexandria. He said, 'Philosophy purges the psyche [ego] and prepares it for Gnosis.'"[45]

Joanna nodded. "Yes. Gnosis is an intellectual pursuit, in a way, because it is a pursuit of wisdom. It must involve some form of contemplation and inquiry. Philosophy can help us find ideas to think about, and it doesn't matter which idea or which method brings us to Gnosis, only that we eventually find God.

"The Gnostic spiritual quest is a path of self knowledge. Not knowledge of the ego self, but of the spiritual self, or the true self. This self is the self of God. Finding God does not happen by accident or serendipity. It is a contemplative journey."

Joanna paused and another hand went up.

"If finding our true self is the ultimate goal, then is this the *truth* that shall set us free? Is this the truth that shall give us *true* freedom?"

Joanna nodded. "I think so. That surely is the test. Freedom for me has nothing to do with laws, restrictions, or the ability to do what I want. I feel more trapped in this body, than behind these walls. The men on the other side of these walls may feel free, but without Gnosis they are lost. How can there be freedom without knowledge of who we are?"

There was silence, then finally another question was asked.

"Can anyone truly have Gnosis? I mean, isn't God an unknowable mystery?"

Joanna smiled. "Of course you can have Gnosis. I hope all of you have Gnosis. While God is the absolute mystery, we can become aware of God and know ourselves to be *part* of God. We can *know* that. We can then grasp the perfection of life, the complete justice of God's unconditional love."

45 Clement of Alexandria, Strom., 6-26.

Joanna paused. "Perhaps the most wonderful thing we can learn is the absolute perfection of God's soul. God may be an unknowable mystery, but I think that God's perfection is knowable. At least *I* feel it as part of my awareness. And if I can grasp the perfection of God's soul, then I can grasp the perfection of my own. And that is a beautiful thing!"

Joanna smiled. "Okay. Off you go. We are finished."

Chapter Seventeen

The Inquisition

From 1234 until 1242, the Inquisition methodically hunted down the remaining Perfecti and their supporters. It was a slow process, since Languedoc was so large, with many towns and villages. Also, there weren't many Perfecti left after the crusade, which made it harder to find the few survivors.

The inquisitors didn't reach Toulouse until 1241. They saved it as the last town to be purged. Toulouse did have a visit from the inquisitors in 1235. However, they were promptly thrown out of town, after they attempted to arrest some of the town leaders.

Once they finished in Toulouse, all that was left was Montségur.

* * * * *

In June 1242, Joanna watched helplessly from behind the fortress walls as the Crusading army finally laid siege to Montségur from the valley below. It was the last Cathar stronghold, and held over two hundred Perfecti, many of whom were the elite leaders of the Cathars. Once it fell, there would be only dozens of Perfecti hidden throughout Languedoc. This was the last stand.

Joanna hurried to find her mother. Entering her mother's small stone room, she could not contain her emotion. "Mother!"

she exclaimed tearfully, "The Crusaders have laid siege to Montségur!"

Blanche arose, wearing her Perfecti brown robe. She had been given the *consolamentum* and become a Perfecti a few years earlier. She hugged her daughter, as Joanna cried on her shoulder. Then they separated and faced each other, still standing.

"Is it over, Mother? Is it really over? We're all that's left!"

"I know, dear. I've always known they were coming. That's why I'm here. I couldn't bear to remain in Laurac and hear of your death.

"It was my influence that led you to become a Perfecti," she continued. "I have always been proud of you for pursuing your heritage. That is why I had to be here with you."

Joanna would not be comforted. "They're going to burn us, aren't they?" she asked fearfully.

Blanche hugged Joanna once more. "Joanna, let's not worry about that. I would gladly jump into the flames to be in God's Kingdom!"

"Yes, of course, Mother. I'm not afraid to die. I meant all of the Perfecti here at Montségur. If we all die, that would be a travesty. The Perfecti here are the Holiest of the Holy."

"I know, my dear. We can only pray that the Perfecti have not lived in vain, that their memory will live on, and perhaps one day be rekindled."

"Mary Magdalene's prophecy?"

Blanche nodded. "It will probably never be as it was, like when you were a little girl and the Perfecti walked the streets through all of Languedoc. God's Holy Apostles preached to the people, and we were at peace, knowing that God was amongst us."

"I fear that all will be lost," Joanna replied dejectedly. "The Catholic Church has no conception of God. They have no idea that God's Spirit dwells within us all. They see humanity as fallen and destined for Hell, when, in fact, we are all destined for God's Kingdom. They have it all wrong!"

Blanche consoled her daughter. "I know, I know, but this knowledge cannot be suppressed forever! Eventually, a generation will arise and reveal the Catholic Church's misbegotten ways. There will come a time when Perfecti once again walk with the spirit of God. The indwelling spirit of God can only be denied for so long."

Joanna's demeanor suddenly changed from dejection to excitement. "You really believe the prophecy, don't you, Mother? That the Gnostics will be purged, yet one day in the distant future they will rise again?"

Blanche nodded and grinned.

"Then we must prepare," Joanna said defiantly. "We could be those Gnostics who rise again. Who is to say what our next life shall be? Maybe we will come back and show the way? I have never thought about death before, but now that I am, I think it just means rebirth. We are going to be reborn as Gnostics."

Blanche nodded. "I agree. I have lessons to learn. My soul has not yet been perfected. I might be called a Perfecti, but I know that I am not really one. I am not enlightened."

"I have an idea, Mother. I am going to have a gathering to prepare everyone for our rebirth. What do you think?"

Blanche immediately supported her. "Of course, my dear. That is an excellent idea. We should prepare for our return!"

"Then let's begin tonight." Joanna was solemn, but resolute.

* * * * *

Over two hundred Perfecti gathered in the great room to listen to Joanna. It was a sea of brown robes, and mostly older faces. Since the war began over thirty years ago, there were very few initiates. Now everyone had reached middle age and beyond. Joanna was actually one of the youngest Perfecti.

Joanna stood in front of one the fireplaces. It was summertime, so there was no fire. Everyone else gathered nearby, and sat down at one of the wooden tables.

"I have an idea," Joanna began in a loud determined voice. "I know that it is odd, and if you do not want to stay and listen, I will understand. The idea is simply that we should prepare, not for death, but for rebirth. We all believe in reincarnation, and my idea is that we should all prepare to come back together—as a group. We can be the prophecy of Mary Magdalene. We can all come back as Gnostics in the distant future, when the time is right."

Joanna paused to let everyone absorb the idea, then scanned the room. But there was only silence.

"Is this a good idea, or is it insanity?" Joanna asked.

"What do you mean by 'prepare'?" Gilbert asked solemnly.

"We should all make a commitment to purify our souls between now and our awaited fate, which will likely be in a few months. While we are purifying our souls, we will ask God to bring us all back together—when the time is right for the Gnostics to rise again."

Joanna paused again.

"What do you mean by 'purify the soul'? How do we achieve this purification?" Gilbert asked.

"Every morning, from tomorrow forward, we will pray to God that we can all incarnate together at the right time. We will each meditate in the morning and consciously connect to the *nous,* to the source of life. We will open up this doorway to the soul, and tap into the purity. Each day, we will bring in a little bit more love into our lives. We will live with a quiet mind—intensely aware of the present—suppressing the chatter of the ego. We will live pure—content, grateful, and generous with our love. We will live out our remaining days in a spiritual stupor.

This way, when we cross over, we will be ready for our next life as a Gnostic.

"If we do it correctly, we will create intense joyfulness, which comes directly from the soul and has nothing to do with this life. If we do it correctly, we can purify the ego, and attain mastery over its control. No longer will any of the deadly sins haunt us.

"Lust will be held at bay, because it can only be fed with imagination and a chattering mind. Wrath will have no chance to get our attention, since we will be consumed with love. Pride is merely a lack of contentment, which we will find every morning and hold diligently. Gluttony is the last thing that should be on our minds during this period. But greed is a tricky one. The ego is going to try and trick us into wanting to live. Greed and contentment are opposite thoughts. Make sure to find your contentment before you leave your room each morning. Sloth will become apparent if you are not meditating vigilantly every day. Now is not the time to be lazy. Envy is like greed, not being content. Do not envy the survivors on the other side of these walls. We Perfecti are closer to God than nearly everyone on this planet. So we hold nothing to envy out there."

"So you are asking us to have a spiritual quest during our remaining days? A quest to reincarnate together as Gnostics?" Gilbert asked quizzically, shaking his head in wonder.

Joanna nodded. "Exactly. This is an opportunity that we should use to prepare for our future. We have to slay our demons and temptations. Life is not about hedonism or nihilism. It is about getting better, maturing as souls. We are here to become pure, to develop mastery over the ego and our prideful ways."

Joanna paused for a response, but the room was silent, so she continued.

"This is our final opportunity for this lifetime. Let's not waste this chance. Let's use it as a mission to accomplish something reverent, something important. Let's come back and resurrect the Gnostics."

Joanna pointed at the wall to her right. "Those aren't our enemies on the other side of that wall, they are ourselves. The same energy that is the source of my soul, is the source of theirs. Have no contempt for them. Be accepting of life. Be considerate, be generous, be enthusiastic, be gentle, be grateful, and be content. Why? Because we are God!

"Now, every morning, meditate on that thought. Open the doorway to the *nous,* and then quiet the mind. Keep it quiet throughout the day, with the pursuit of adding love to your consciousness. Learn to resonate love. That is why we are here. That is the meaning of life. While you are resonating love, ask God to bring us all back together. I know that He will if we all ask.

"Jesus spoke of being consumed by fire. He wasn't talking about death. No, he was speaking about love and its power. Love is what he was talking about! Every morning is a new chance to be consumed by that fire of love. It is a new chance to be content and grateful for that fire. This fire of love is what energizes our soul. We can bring more love into our lives, and then resonate and vibrate higher. That should be our goal over these last few months.

"The Crusaders are going to throw all of us into the flames, but I want you to be prepared. When you go to the flames, I want you to be thinking of the flames of love that are burning in your heart. Have no fear. The bonfire of Crusaders are merely the doorway back home. The flames cannot burn your soul. Take your mind, and place it in your soul, in the *nous*. You will feel no pain as you transition home."

Joanna stopped, and looked slowly at each face around her.

One of the female Perfecti rose and put her palms together in the sign of prayer and thankfulness. Soon all of the Perfecti were on their feet, acknowledging Joanna with the sign of prayer.

Joanna smiled, and put her palms together, too, as a symbol of gratitude and togetherness. The room of Perfecti agreed to take up her spiritual quest as a group. Over the next nine months they would spend most of their time meditating, fasting and preparing their souls for the return home.

* * * * *

Nine months later, Montségur finally surrendered. Joanna went to inform her mother, inside the monastery. She was in her room.

"Mother," Joanna said solemnly, "Gilbert has surrendered. We are completely out of food and water. The Crusaders are here to take us down the hill."

"What day is it?" Blanche asked without emotion, tired and weary.

"It's Monday, March 16*th*, 1243. Why?"

"I didn't want to be burned on a Sunday. Have the Crusaders started the fire yet?"

Joanna nodded. "It's a large bonfire. I think they're going to burn us together."

"How many Perfecti are here?"

"Gilbert told me two hundred and ten."

"I am ready," Blanche replied. "I have said my peace to God."

"Can you walk down the hill, Mother?"

"Yes. I am old, but I can still walk. I'll be fine."

"Oh, Mother, I wish this day would not have come," Joanna said, close to crying.

"It's okay, Joanna. We are going to God's Kingdom. You know that. We have prepared for this day for months. Today isn't the day to weep. We should be joyous. We are going home."

"Oh, Mother, I want to be joyous. Every morning I have meditated and prepared, but my spirit wants to stay and preach to the people. I'm not afraid to die, but it is sad to see the Gnostics go."

"Joanna, I know," Blanche said, hugging her now weeping daughter.

"Right now, right this second," Blanche said, with a resolved inner strength, "I want you to forgive God and accept your fate. Let us walk to the fire together and jump in of our own accord. Before this day is over, we will be in God's Kingdom. For that, we should be grateful."

Joanna finally stopped weeping, and actually smiled at the prospect of their new adventure together.

"Mother, I love you so much!" she said. "Yes, I will do as you ask. No more weeping and complaining. Let us go to God's Kingdom with dignity. The Crusaders will not see fear on my face. Instead, they will see a smile of happiness."

Blanche grinned. "Now *that* is the fearless Perfecti daughter that I raised!"

* * * * *

After the slow hike to the bottom of the hill, the long line of Perfecti—all dressed in their ubiquitous brown robes—queued in a single file toward the bonfire.

About ten feet from the bonfire, two Crusaders would grab the next Perfecti in line, bind his or her hands and feet, and toss them into the fire. But many of the Perfecti broke from the queue and ran into the flames on their own.

When Blanche and Joanna were within twenty feet, they both ran into the flames together, holding hands. The Crusaders simply stood by and watched, mystified. Each woman had a smile on her face as they jumped into the flames together.

* * * * *

A few days later, at Château Narbonnais, Antoine, now reaching old age, went to inform Raymond VII about Montségur.

"My Lord, Montségur has fallen. All of the Perfecti were burned."

Raymond VII immediately bowed his head in mourning, stricken by the devastating news—even though he had known it was coming.

He was now middle aged, with nothing left but his castle and a few servants. He had already resigned himself to living out his remaining days, in utter defeat, at Château Narbonnais. Without his lands or his mercenary army, he had no more power.

"I let them down, Antoine, when I signed the Treaty of Paris. I should have fought further. I should *never* have agreed to terms!"

"My Lord, there was nothing you could have done. Your enemies were too powerful. If you had resisted the treaty, it would have made no difference."

"You humor me, Antoine. My father would have *never* surrendered. He would have died for the Perfecti! Now what is left? The Catholics! The people of Languedoc are not Catholics! I despise them! They have taken my lands *and* our God. The pure ones are gone now! All that is left are defiled priests who want our tithes!"

At first, Antoine did not know how to answer. He had never seen the Lord so angry.

At last he replied, soothingly, "One day, my Lord, the Catholics will meet their demise. One day there will no longer be a Pope."

"Antoine, I hope you are right," countered Raymond VII, finally calming down. "They deserve that, after what they have done here."

An uncomfortable silence hung heavily over them.

Antoine grinned, and tried to lighten the mood. "The Perfecti will simply be reborn and will preach again. After all, they believe in reincarnation."

Raymond laughed. "Antoine, now we're dreaming."

Antoine smiled. "But it's a good dream, my Lord."

Epilogue

In 1243, when Montségur fell, the Cathars were nearly eliminated from Languedoc. The Inquisition remained for several more decades, finishing the job and ensuring that the Cathars did not reappear.

There was one last gasp for Languedoc in the late thirteenth century, when a Perfecti named Pierre Autier began preaching in Foix. His magnetism quickly invigorated a small Cathar movement. Autier was burned in 1310, and a ruthless Inquisition from 1318 until 1326 made sure that there were no more Cathars in Languedoc.

The fourteenth century was the last time that early Christian Gnostic groups existed anywhere in Europe. There were small numbers of Cathars in northern Italy and other parts of Europe; however, they were being persecuted by the Catholic Church and kept in hiding. By the end of the fourteenth century, the Catholic Church had succeeded in completely eliminating their influence.

Those Gnostics that did exist in Europe, from that period onward, usually worshipped alone and in secret. It should be mentioned that there were dozens of early Christian Gnostic groups that emerged after Christ's crucifixion—in addition to the Cathars. Some of these groups, such as the Manicheans, Simonians, Valentinians, and Bogomils (who existed during the time of the Cathars), were quite large and dispersed over a wide area of the Middle East, the Mediterranean area, and Eastern Europe.

When the Catholic Church became the legal Church of Rome, after the First Council of Nicaea in 325 AD, all of these Gnostic groups were outlawed and persecuted. If it were not for this persecution, there would have been a much larger Gnostic influence today.

The Nag Hammadi Scrolls, found in 1945, offer the best glimpse into how Christian spirituality would be today if the Gnostics Scriptures had been included in the Bible. Instead, these scriptures were destroyed and kept from the public. Today we know what they reveal: Jesus' teachings were Gnostic, and have little resemblance to the Christian Churches that arose in his name.

CPSIA information can be obtained
at www.ICGtesting.com
Printed in the USA
FFOW01n1802071115
18333FF